A History of Slovak Literature

In spite of its richness and long history, Slovak literature is one of the least-known Slavic literatures in the English-speaking world. Few translations of Slovak works exist and until now there has been no systematic English-language history of this field. *A History of Slovak Literature* provides an excellent introduction to this important but overlooked body of writing.

Starting with the Great Moravian period, Peter Petro surveys one thousand years of Slovak literature. He examines the medieval, renaissance, baroque, classical, romantic, realist, and modern periods and highlights the contributions of such writers as Nedožerský, Tranovský, Papánek, Šafárik, Kollár, Záborský, Vajanský, Hviezdoslav, Kukučín, Hronský, Tatarka, and Rúfus.

Like Czech, Polish, and Ukrainian writing, Slovak literature transcended the merely literary to become an influential political and cultural tool: Slovak writers and poets played an important role in promoting and protecting the culture and language of their people against invading cultures. *A History of Slovak Literature* will be a welcome addition to the field of Slavic studies.

PETER PETRO is associate professor of Russian, East European, and comparative literature, University of British Columbia.

ISBN 0-7735-1311-6 (cloth)
ISBN 0-7735-1402-3 (paper)
Legal deposit fourth quarter 1995
Bibliothèque nationale du Québec

Printed in Canada on acid-free paper
Paperback edition 1996

Published simultaneously in the European Union by Liverpool University Press.

This book has been published with the help of a grant from the Canadian Federation for the Humanities, using funds provided by the Social Sciences and Humanities Research Council of Canada.

McGill-Queen's University Press is grateful to the Canada Council for support of its publishing program.

Canadian Cataloguing in Publication Data

Petro, Peter
A history of Slovak literature
Includes bibliographical references and index.
ISBN 0-7735-1311-6
1. Slavic literature – History and criticism. I. Title.
PG5401.P48 1995 891.8'709 C95-900408-4

This book was typeset by Typo Litho Composition Inc.
in 10/12 Baskerville.

Contents

Acknowledgments

I would like to thank Kevin Michael Grace for his assistance with the final draft of my manuscript: his editorial skill, criticism, and erudition were as appreciated as his friendship.

I am also very thankful for the support my project has received from the Cultural Foundation of the Slovak World Congress and its directors. My inquiries to Matica slovenská, in Bratislava, were promptly answered, through I do regret that I did not have the opportunity to do research in its library.

I am very grateful for the practical help of Father Félix Litva, SJ, professor at the Gregorian University in Rome, without whose personal intercession the bulk of my manuscript would not have been written. Father Sebastian Košút's indomitable optimism and helpfulness and my conversations with Stano Dusík in Florence were both extremely helpful. Finally, I would like to thank Dr. Imrich Kružliak, who suggested this project to me and believed that I could execute it.

Much of the last chapter was originally presented as a lecture to a conference on Czechoslovakia 1918–88, on October 28, 1988, in Toronto. Josef Škvorecky's kind and encouraging comments were extremely helpful, as were the suggestions of Professor H. Gordon Skilling. Much of what I have to say about Hronský, Šikula, the surrealists, and the 1960s appeared in the periodical *Slovakia* (1982–83). I received encouragement in the writing of these articles from Professor Bogdan Czaykowski, of the University of British Columbia, who supported my interest in Slovak literature.

All translations are mine. For texts quoted from well-known classics, I assume standard editions and do not provide citations. Occasionally, I provide a source quotation, as an example or when the text has extra-literary implications.

Preface

Those who read the story of Slovak literature may be compared to the old rafters on the river Váh. They made their rafts upstream, almost at the source of the river, high in the mountains, where the rivers are born. When they first launched their craft, they sped down the river. With each part of their journey, the river became wider, as the heretofore constricting valleys gave way to a wide, open plain. There was more to see, and what there was appeared more complex and more difficult to make out from the middle of the river. Finally, they arrived at the mouth of the Váh, where it joins the Danube. The Váh was a mature river here, its waters not that different from those of the bigger, cosmopolitan Danube. And so it is with Slovak literature: in its maturity, it is a distinguished member of the European family of literatures.

Slovak literature itself can be compared to Cinderella: the beauty, ability, and potential for fame are there, but it is unknown, or at any rate less well known than it deserves to be – to the English-speaking word, at any rate. Few translations exist to remedy this lack of knowledge. Nevertheless, the world is beginning to take notice of Slovak literature, as evidenced by the international conference, organized by the University of London's School of Slavonic and Eastern European Studies, entitled "Slovak Prose After 1954" (1987). The first to deal with this literature and a fitting testimonial to its growing importance, the conference dealt with more than a dozen very talented Slovak novelists. This is a step in the right direction. The next step should be systematic translation of the best Slovak literature, past and present.

This work is intended as a guide for those who would like to be introduced to Slovak literature, as well as Slavists. Knowing this literature also means getting acquainted with the people who have lived for over a millennium right in the centre of Europe, whose culture and language have survived against all odds, and whose literature is in a sense unique – for in it we see, as in a mirror, a reflection of the unceasing battle for a subtle balance between the great forces of East and West, North and South. Above all, as a great Slovak poet, Hugolín Gavlovič, said, "There is no greater wealth than literature." With this kind of wealth, such considerations as the size of the country and its political success or failure do not really matter. What does matter is the expression of genius through the medium of literature. This book is an invitation to meet this genius.

A History of Slovak Literature

Introduction

Because Slovak literature has a millennium of history behind it, I shall begin my study with the ancient, sometimes contradictory, often incomplete record of the Great Moravian period. Indeed, the standard Slovak histories of literature begin with this epoch, though they do not dwell on it at great length. Alternatively, I could begin at the end of the eighteenth century and cover only the last two hundred years (1780–1990). A far greater amount of Slovak literature appeared in this period than did in the roughly eight hundred years that preceded it. In *History of Slovak Literature* (*Dejiny literatúry slovenskej*, 1890) written at the end of the nineteenth century, Jaroslav Vlček stated that Slovak literature was one hundred years old, for what remained of the pagan times was but a faint shadow and writing in the first centuries of Christianity was in Latin, while from the fifteenth to the eighteenth centuries Slovak literary production was formally linked with the Czech.

To get a more complex and satisfactory answer, we must turn to the beginning of the flowering of Slovak literature, in the first half of the nineteenth century. This flowering, though certainly stimulated by the ideology of nationalism emanating from France and Germany, was not a creation *ex nihilo.* Each of the great writers of the Slovak national revival could point to a predecessor; the predecessors could do likewise. We can follow this chain of literary tradition back to one time: *Moravia Magna,* the Great Moravian period.

If it makes sense to adopt this chronological approach, we must also face another problem that may seem rather surprising: much Slovak literature before the eighteenth century was not written in Slovak.

Thus, before discussing medieval literature, I shall give a brief overview of the historical and linguistic background of Slovakia, with a note on the influence of the Christian missionaries.

HISTORICAL AND LINGUISTIC BACKGROUND

Slovakia is a West Slavic nation, and its religion, language, and literature reflect its geographical situation. No less important than this geographical fact is the historical fact that from a position of relative eminence as the main constituent element of the first Slavic state – the Great Moravian Empire – Slovakia disappeared, politically speaking, from the map, after the Magyars defeated it at the beginning of the tenth century (907) and absorbed it into the kingdom of Hungary. It reappeared again as a part of a new state, Czecho-Slovakia, in 1918, but this state broke up in 1939; between 1939 and 1945, the Slovak Republic existed. After the war, the prewar state was re-established minus the Trans-Carpathian Ukraine (also called Ruthenia), which was ceded to the Soviet Union. Since 1993, following the breakup of the Czech and Slovak Federation, Slovakia has been an independent republic, with a population of six million.

At the time of its greatest extension, at the end of the ninth century, the Great Moravian Empire included, apart from Slovakia, Bohemia, southern Poland, parts of the Ukraine, Serbia, Croatia, Hungary, and Austria.

One consequence of the loss of political independence was the lack of a literary language until the end of the eighteenth century. This does not mean that until the Slovak language was officially codified, in 1843, nobody actually used it *in writing* (it is understood that Slovak was always the medium of *oral* communication). However, it was more convenient, during this period, for people to write in the language that they were taught at school or in church: Latin, German, Hungarian, or Czech. Therefore, from the point of view of language, the history of Slovak literature can be divided into three periods: Old Slavic, the time of the Great Moravian Empire; multilingual, until the end of the eighteenth century; and *literary Slovak,* which is further divided into "Bernolák Slovak" (1787–1843), and "Štúr Slovak" (1843 to the present). Anton Bernolák (1762–1813) proposed a West Slovak dialect for the literary language, but it did not find wide acceptance. Ľudovít Štúr's (1815–56) Central Slovak dialect was codified in 1843, and it is the basis of the modern Slovak language, with minor orthographic and grammatical changes.

It is impossible, however, to overestimate the literary, cultural, political, and, above all, religious significance of the Byzantine Christian mission of saints Cyril and Methodius, who brought their own alphabet into the Great Moravian Empire in the year 863, and who transcribed the liturgical texts into the language spoken by medieval Slovaks. Thus, paradoxically, there was a literary language on the Slovak territory a millennium before the advent of "Bernolák Slovak."

It is the multilingual period that causes the greatest difficulties in obvious linguistic identification of any national literature (for example, Germany, Austria, and Switzerland share a language, but each has a separate literary history). If a Slovak were to write in Latin, nobody would question the fact that he is a Slovak writer and not a Roman one; the difficulty arises when a Slovak writer uses Czech, German, or Hungarian. The solution advocated by contemporary literary historiographers in Slovakia is to share such authors with the literature of the language they used, particularly if their work played a significant role in the history of both literatures, as is the case for some Slovak authors claimed by the Czech, Hungarian, and Austrian literatures.

For those wishing to acquaint themselves with the treasury of Slovak literature in Slovak, the period following the codification of the language, in 1843, is of particular importance, since few would venture to read Old Slavic, Latin, German, Hungarian, or biblical Czech. Nevertheless, many important works were written before 1843 in an accessible Slovak with some Bohemisms, in substantially Slovakized Czech, and in Czech. Even if they were written in a less accessible language, sometimes the very nature and significance of some earlier works demands that we at least take a look at them.

THE MISSION OF SAINTS CYRIL AND METHODIUS

Since we lack any definitive evidence of literary works written before the mission of saints Cyril and Methodius, the written record starts with them. At the outset, we must distinguish between the religious and cultural mission of the Apostles to the Slavs and the various later (nineteenth- and twentieth-century) uses and abuses of the mission in support of nationalistic, ideological, and political claims, however justified or dubious.

Saints Cyril and Methodius came from Thessalonica, known to the Slavs as Solun, in Byzantium, at the request of Rastislav, the ruler of the Great Moravian Empire. The reason was that Rastislav wanted the Christian faith to be introduced in a language that the people could understand. He also wanted to keep the Franks, whence some previous missions had come, at a distance, in order to achieve a balance of the two Christian powers.

Great Moravia had a rich cultural life even before this mission, and Christian missions from the Frankish Empire had reached the territory long before. This posits the question of a certain clash of cultural influences, albeit both of them Christian: Rome versus Byzantium. There is a danger that such an interpretation is anachronistic: a succession of popes supported the mission of saints Cyril and Methodius and even elevated the language of the Great Moravian Empire to the status of a liturgical language on a par with Hebrew, Greek, and Latin.

Saints Cyril and Methodius were well-educated brothers from the family of a high imperial administrator, and both had shown unusual talent and abilities from an early age. The elder brother, Methodius, gave up the office of *archont*, or administrator, of a province with a sizeable Slavic population in order to enter a monastery. The younger brother, Cyril (also known as Constantine, Cyril being his monastic name), was an ordained priest who refused an important political office. He, too, secretly entered a monastery at the Black Sea. It was with some difficulty that he was found and pressed into diplomatic service and lecturing in philosophy at the university in Constantinople. Thus, their education, talents, and experience made Methodius and Cyril ideal candidates to undertake the mission to the Slavs. They willingly did so and prepared themselves well, designing an alphabet with which they could transcribe the Gospels and liturgical texts before they set out, in 863, for Great Moravia.

The translation of the Bible has an absolutely essential significance for literature in every nation. The literary quality of the Holy Scripture – its poetry, means of expression, superior rhetorics, style, and strong epic element – make its translation a literary event of the greatest magnitude. At the same time, in Great Moravia such an act must have been devastating for the flourishing pagan culture, for Christianity largely destroyed it, absorbing certain natural rites. In Great Moravia, Slovak literature received a powerful charge from the clash of pagan and Christian cultures. This was followed by another clash: that of the two competing Christian traditions, Roman and Byzantine, struggling for superiority in this borderline area. The Old Slavic language had to give way to Latin after the area came under the control of Roman hierarchy, which tried to marginalize the Byzantine influence; the latter survived only in the liturgy of the Slovak Catholics of the Byzantine rite. The wider cultural significance and historical ramifications of the Christian mission of saints Cyril and Methodius are beyond the scope of this work.

Today, after many political changes, Slovak culture is solidly Western. It is a part of a wider Central European, pan-European, or even global context. Western culture and civilization are considered to be a

Slovak cultural heritage, the result of the Christian influence built partly on the Graeco-Roman cultural edifice. As Štefan Krčméry, the most brilliant Slovak literary historiographer, wrote, "Christianity brought a deep and systematic spiritual life in whose rhythm all of Europe began slowly to unify. In Slavdom, a special role in this process fell to the Slovaks" (1976, 1:53).

It may be difficult to assess the impact of the mission of saints Cyril and Methodius on the Slovak language itself. At the same time, it is hardly contentious to assume that without their mission, Great Moravia would have become a Frankish preserve with a dominant Latin influence. This would have seriously undermined the chances for survival of the Slovak language.

1 Medieval Literature (800–1467)

Christianity made itself felt most strongly in medieval literature. If we conceive of the medieval period as sandwiched between pagan times and the Renaissance, we may see it as a time of an admirable unity, harmony, and homogeneity of civil, religious, wordly, and cultural sensibilities and of a faith the strength of which gave us cathedrals, Gregorian chants, and a unique, often anonymous, but far-reaching artistic creativity.

Medieval literature accepts the Christian transcendence of the world, and it is from this perspective (*sub specie aeternitatis*) that it describes the world. The allegory, symbolism, and what Dante called the "anagogic" or transcendent, mystical approach to reality serve a definite purpose: to emphasize the belief that our world is but a reflection (as in a glass darkly) of the heavenly one.

It is accepted by Slovak historiographers that the medieval period lasted for some seven centuries in Slovak literature, from 800 to 1500 (see Pišút 1984). It began with the alphabet of Cyril, devised following the Greek alphabet, and a small group of Old Slavic authors – Cyril, Methodius, and Clement (Kliment) – active in Great Moravia, comprising the seed that eventually fertilized the literature of other Slavic nations. Cyril translated the liturgical books (*trebnik*), the breviary (*časoslov*), the *Great Moravian Legal Codex*, and the missal (*služebnik*). Cyril and Methodius translated the New Testament (*Nový zákon*), the Psalms (*Psalterium*), the Acts of the Apostles, and the *oktoich* (*osmiglasnik*). In addition, Cyril wrote *Proglas* (Prologue to the Gospels) and *Praise in Honour of St Gregory of Nazianzus*. These are exclusively religious texts, but they stand at the very beginning of Slavic – and Slovak – literature. A little-appreciated fact bears repeating: secular culture follows sacred culture. This pattern holds true here: in the fragment of Cyril's *Prologue to the Gospels* (eleventh–twelfth century) are literary-critical passages.

Methodius was the translator of almost all of the Old Testament, as well as the author of the *Adhortation* (a copy is extant from the eleventh century), a sermon quite possibly aimed at Svätopluk, the greatest, but also the most controversial, of the Great Moravian rulers.

The closest collaborator of the saints was Clement, a native of Great Moravia. *The Life of Constantine* (870) and *The Life of Methodius* (885–894), both ascribed to him, were written in Old Church Slavonic and are without any doubt the most important literary texts of the Great Moravian period. When Methodius's disciples were forced to leave Great Moravia, they enriched Bulgaria with their literary work. While their departure hurt the cause of Slavic culture in Great Moravia, it provided a pioneering and lasting contribution to the whole of Slavdom.

Apart from written literature, there was always oral literature, or folk literature, in such genres as fairy-tales, songs, proverbs, riddles, fables, and anecdotes. It is here that one finds the truest and oldest expression of universal literary structures. Today, they are submerged in the detritus of professional literature and, worse, wrenched away from their original, intended audience, surviving not in people's hearts, but in library stacks. Comparative studies of the migration of fairy-tales show the process of mutual enrichment of national folk literatures; evidence of their influence is visible in the archetypal stories from which the various national folk traditions borrow.

In Slovak folk literature, the oldest commonly accepted songs have to do with seasonal rites of pagan origin, such as "Morena, Morena, Who Did You Die For?," "Jano, Jano Vajanuo," and "Hoja Dunda, hoja." Though they show some traces of distortion, the consensus is that they fulfilled some ritual function. For instance, Morena, a puppet personification of winter, was carried on a stick in a procession and thrown into water at the end of winter, symbolizing the death of that season and the coming of spring.

With the fall of the Great Moravian Empire began another period highlighting the role of oral literature, a period about which very little is known. The discontinuity from an established Byzantine-influenced cultural situation must have been difficult to overcome. Culturally, the defeat meant the end of Svätopluk's clever balancing act between the Franks, Byzantium, and Rome. Henceforth, Christian Western European culture prevailed, swept in with the creation of monasteries, church schools, universities, and libraries, along with religious communities dedicated to its dissemination. The Benedictines, particularly well known for their civilizing influence, had established their house in Zobor, near Nitra, by the end of the tenth century. For the next thousand years, until the end of the nineteenth century, almost all outstanding Slovak authors came from the ranks of clergy – first Catholic and then, after the Reformation, Protestant.

PROSE

Legends, blending artistic and historical elements, were the most popular medieval genre. It is a mistake to judge them against our standards of historicity and veracity, since their aim was not history as such, but spiritual advancement of the reader. Nonetheless, their historical basis should not be dismissed, especially in the absence of contrary evidence.

Of those that are extant, one is based on a source from Slovakia, *The Legend of St Svorad and Benedikt* (1064–70), by Maurus (1001–70), a bishop of Pätikostolie circa 1036. Three other legends, with a Hungarian background, deal with the story of St Stephen: *The Major Legend* (late eleventh century), *The Minor Legend* (early twelfth century), and *Hartvik's Legend* (also early twelfth century).

The Legend of St Svorad and Benedikt depicts the lives of hermits and monks. Svorad, who took the name Andrew when he became a monk, was a native of Liptov, in Slovakia. He entered the Benedictine monastery of St Hypolitus in Zobor, near Nitra. Seeking a more ascetic life, he left the monastic community to live as a hermit at Skalka, near Trenčín. His disciple, Benedikt, followed him, but he was captured by robbers and killed, and his body was thrown into the river Váh.

The legend is a very impressive account of an exceptional life. Much of it is written following a pattern common to all legends dealing with the lives of the saints: the person is idealized, and so on. Indeed, love of hard, physical work, true *askesis,* combined with fasting and physical discomfort, are features common to many, if not all, saints who seek to overcome the temporal in order better to develop the spiritual. Still, this legend yields a remarkable and memorable story of a modest, self-effacing character who hailed from a simple peasant background. What is most interesting is Svorad's exemplary Christian compassion for the robbers. Thus, it is not surprising to discover that one of the miracles ascribed to him was the resurrection of a hanged robber:

> In Nitra, they hanged a certain criminal. When, with the mercy of God, he was saved, he came to Abbot Phillip and told him that he had been saved through

the intercession of the Blessed Andrew. He related that when he was being sentenced, he called upon Andrew's name, and when they were stringing him up, the Blessed Andrew supported him with his own hands. When all present thought he was dead and went home, Andrew untied him and let him go.

The Hungarian legends deal with the important events of Hungarian history, such as the struggle of St Stephen to convert some of his more recalcitrant warriors to Christianity. However, since the time that the Slovak territory was absorbed into the kingdom of Hungary, the history of the latter naturally included that of the former.

The authors of the medieval period used some writing tools, including handbooks such as the celebrated *Synonyms*, by Isidor de Seville (560–636) and Roland de Passageri's (d. 1300) notary handbook *Summa notaria* (1260). Some very influential sermons, such as the homilies of Bartholomew of Munsterberg (1448), who comments on the wars of the Hussite Brethren, and Martin Ciwisch's sermons on the Black Death (1360), are an important part of the literary heritage of this period. Among the lighter, more entertaining works were legends directly or indirectly taken from the international treasury *The Golden Legend* (*Legenda aurea*, before 1260), collected by the Italian Dominican priest Jacobus da Varagine (1230–98). Copies of this anthology were found in Slovakia. Many biblical stories were turned into diverting or instructional reading, and there were even legends about the Great Moravian saints (*Cyril and Methodius*, 1423), as well as Czech ones (*St-Adalbert*, 1340).

A number of Slovak authors were involved with the Czech Hussite cause. Lukáš (d. 1424), from Nové Mesto, was a student at Charles University, in Prague, and later became a Taborite priest in Písek. His tractati and polemics are not extant.

SLOVAKIZED CZECH AND LATIN

Also important to the Slovak literary heritage are the texts written in Slovakized Czech, a linguistic phenomenon that appeared in the fourteenth century, and in Latin. "Slovakized Czech" describes the use of the Czech language by a Slovak author (in the absence of codified – literary – Slovak) who often inserts Slovak words into the text. These texts are easy to identify. Sometimes they use Slovak words that are not found in Czech, and at other times they improperly use Czech words. The reason for this is obvious. Czechs had a literary language; Slovaks, due to their loss of political independence to Hungary early in the tenth century, did not. The easiest language to understand in the surrounding area was Czech. Some Slovaks studied, and lectured, at the

Czech university in Prague; there were other contacts as well. Nevertheless, Slovakized Czech was but one of several languages Slovaks used for literary purposes, others being Latin and, later, German and Hungarian. Some legends entered Slovakia in the form of Slovakized Czech, such as the well-known *Legend of St George.*

The common treasury of contemporary literature available in Western Europe freely circulated in Latin and was well known in Slovakia. Such works as the *Gesta Romanorum* (Strassburg, 1499) and the *Fables of Aesop* (Venice, 1494) were available in *incunabula.* The availability of theoretical works, such as Robert de Basevon's *Summa or the Art of Writing* (1455) and *Modus praedicandi* (1462–73), as well as Christoph Petschmessingsloer's *Laudes arti poeticae* (1461), was also a factor in the education of Slovak authors.

Petschmessingsloer was a native of Levoča who studied in Cracow, Poland. He was very attracted to the work of the Roman satirist Juvenal, and his above-mentioned work is actually an introduction to Juvenal's satires. His sources were ancient and not-so-ancient authorities: Aristotle, Cicero, Juvenal, Boethius, Alan ab Insulis, and Thomas Aquinas. True to the medieval world-view, he considered poetry to be the result of divine inspiration. Nevertheless, he realized that it was an *art* with rules that had to be mastered. His work is a handbook on the writing of poetry.

DRAMA

In the medieval period, the most widespread form of drama was the mystery. Mysteries originated in the Christian liturgy, particularly the dramatic account of the Paschal mystery, the crucifixion and the resurrection of Jesus Christ.

The first theatres were the churches. The actors were priests, performing in Latin. Over time, the plays evolved into wordly spectacles that were no longer suitable for the house of God. The number of plays grew as well, and so laypeople became the actors and the vernacular was introduced. Of special significance for Slovak literature was the *igric,* or wandering minstrel. Vagrant clerics and students making their way from the universities of Cracow to Padua, Bologna, Paris, and Prague were also among the performers. They would act in the interludes, the light, entertaining intermezzi between the acts of the Passion-play. Another type of play portrayed the dramatized lives of saints, such as St Dorothea and St Catharine.

The Igric

This type of performer resembles the medieval figures of Minnesinger, the troubadour, and the poets of courtly love. According to some accounts, the *igric* was often a less glamorous figure. He may have been a simple mime or a clownish singer. Nevertheless, the role of the *igric* appears not to have been comical in essence by any means. On the contrary, in some interpretation, the *igric* appears as almost a prophet, a *vates*, as the gifts of poetry and invention were considered, at the time, not unlike the gift of clairvoyance. In any case, both kinds of inspiration were, by definition, divine. Thus, the *igric* is a profoundly ambiguous figure. How much of this ambiguity can be ascribed to the still unsettled cultural environment due to the clash of the Byzantine and Western cultures can only be surmised. A clue may be provided by the figure of the Russian *skomorokh*, also a wandering performer. If the two were in any way related, the Byzantine connection would be strengthened.

The literary significance of the *igric* is clear, for he is among the first secular representatives of culture and literature, which, until his arrival, was almost without exception church sponsored and oriented. We have descriptions of two *igrics*: one residing in the Bratislava Castle and the other in the Zvoleň Castle (both in the fifteenth century). In fact, the *igric* may have been a member of the lower nobility: the kind of education and the ability to comport himself properly in the castle surroundings demanded a level of sophistication difficult to imagine in a serf or a simple townsman.

The *igric* was also the ideal raconteur, providing a link between the world of folk literature and the beginnings of prose. It is true that many fairy-tales, to take one genre, come from foreign sources – old Egyptian, Hindu, or Greek. As collections such as *Gesta Romanorum*, *Arabian Nights*, and the *Deccamerone* suggest, there is an incredible amount of migration of good stories across national boundaries. Apart from such borrowings, there is a corpus of folk literature that originates in Slovakia, which, however, was collected not in the medieval period, but much later.

Thus, although the medieval period has left us with few names, for it was an age of anonymous authors and the *igric*, we do have many texts – legends, interludes, and, above all, a strong folk literature.

2 The Renaissance (1467–1636)

As the European cultural phenomenon that determined much of the modern sensibility and ran counter to the many beliefs of the medieval period, the Renaissance is still a controversial movement. In hindsight, particularly in the positivist interpretation of that age common in the nineteenth century, there developed a myth of the Renaissance as the conqueror of the Dark Ages, the victory of the progressive against the primitive mentality. This is increasingly difficult to justify today, in the age of relativism, when anthropologists have disposed of the concept of the primitive man.

One can say in defence of medieval man that he was a viceroy in his universe, which he knew was wisely controlled by God, and, whatever vicissitudes befell him, there was still the final certitude that the misfortune and suffering in this vale of tears would inevitably improve his lot in the next life. Although it can be said that much was good about the Renaissance, it cannot be said that it strengthened man in this key certitude – that it gave him a stronger faith with which to face the blows he increasingly had to bear, or that it promoted wordly or religious unity.

The pluralism of the Renaissance – the play of contradictory ideas, the freedom to experiment, the "humanization" – had an ugly side: the destruction of the unified vision of the world; the gradual polarization of man; his atomization as a social creature; and, as Jacob Burckhardt showed, the creation of a split personality. This was the ultimate and individualized complement to the division that occurred in society. Therefore, we see medieval man as a being who ordered and integrated his experiences into a system that always made sense. He was also integrated into society: there was no division between the man in the family, the man in the world, the man in the work-place, the man in the church, and the man of God. All of these divisions appeared after the Renaissance.

In Slovakia, the Renaissance and humanism, the philosophy that underpinned it, arrived during a particularly trying time. The territory was threatened by attacks by the Turks to the south, particularly after the defeat at Mohács in 1526. They captured Budapest, so the capital of the kingdom of Hungary was moved to Bratislava (then known as Pozsonyi, in Hungarian, and Pressburg, in German). The suffering that the Turkish incursions brought to Slovakia was horrible, the plunderings devastating. To this day, one may see the silent witnesses – the burned-out shells of once-proud castles, beautiful repositories of cultural artifacts and libraries – and contemplate what might have been had they been preserved. But more damaging to the national soul in the long run, particularly in Slovakia's case, were the divisions and wars caused by the Reformation and Counter-Reformation at the end of the sixteenth and the beginning of the seventeenth centuries. The religious civil war dragged on and, in a sense, never ended, even if the bloodletting did finally stop, because the religious divisions were never healed. As Krčméry has said apropos of the guilt of both parties in the conflict – and he was a Protestant pastor – "We cannot blame each other, and if we could, then always both" (1:172).

The aim of the Renaissance was a noble one: to bring the human personality to a higher level, one associated with Graeco-Roman civilization, a paradox – looking back in order to go forward – based on a peculiar interpretation of the nature of antiquity. This thrust was combined with the discoveries of Nicholas Copernicus (1473–1543) and Galileo Galilei (1564–1642), which comprised a radical break with medieval cosmology and thus permanently altered the way human beings view themselves.

Humanists collected, studied, and interpreted the works of Virgil, Horace, Homer, Juvenal, Aristotle, Plato, and others, and used this classical literature as a model for their own work. The thorough study of Latin (in which most of the classics were read) led to improvements in written expression in contemporary Latin, which was used in the Hungarian kingdom, and hence also in Slovakia, not only for literary but also for administrative, educational, and religious purposes.

Unlike medieval literature, the literature of the Renaissance stressed the happy, sensual, physical experiences of man versus nature, man versus human community, and, above all, man and woman. The level of literary expression was tempered and lowered, suggesting the influence of townfolk and the lower nobility, as was only natural during the

Reformation, since the religious question was a classless question: it involved all believers, irrespective of their background.

From roughly the beginning of the sixteenth century until about halfway through the eighteenth century, the literary Renaissance was ushered in by two separate influences: the German influence of Martin Luther (1483–1546) and the Italian influence encouraged by King Mathias Corvinus (1443–90). The latter founded the first university in Slovakia, the Academia Istropolitana in Bratislava, in 1467, a fitting date for the beginning of the Renaissance in Slovakia. Later, in 1635, the Jesuits opened the Catholic university in Trnava. It was the age of learned societies charged with spreading humanistic and Renaissance ideas, and of the building of private libraries (Zachariáš Rohožník-Mošovský's library in Nitra, for example). It was also the age of the printed book; the first Slovak book was Vašek Zaleský's *The Book of Oaths* ..., published in 1561.

Slovakized Czech was beginning to be used more and more as an administrative and a legal language. It was also the language of some outstanding literary works of the period.

As in the previous period, religious poetry was one of the main genres. Much of it was written as song lyrics for church services. Thus, the most significant authors of old Slovak literature were religious-song lyricists: Ján Silván (1493–1573), who wrote *New Songs to Seven Psalms of Repentance and other Psalms* (1571, 1578), Eliáš Láni (1570–1618), the author of ten songs and a prayer (1597–1616), and Vavrinec Benedikt Nedožerský (1555–1615), the author of *Aliquot psalmorum Davidicorum paraphrasis rhytmometrica, lyrico carmine ad imitationem Latinorum primum attentata* (Some psalms in a Czech song in the manner of Latin verses newly introduced and published, 1606).

Silván paraphrased David's *Psalms* to suit the melodies of popular folk-songs such as "O Muráňskom Zámku" (About the Muráň Castle). These psalms were a fitting vehicle for Silván's intimate lyrical disposition, filled with Renaissance elements. There is an entire spectrum of songs, with subjects ranging from the worldly desire for a good wife to the deep suffering of a man battling with his own weak nature. Poems dealing with the ideas of Christian mortification appear alongside poems celebrating natural human desires. This can be interpreted as an example of the clash of old and new thinking – the struggle between medieval and Renaissance world-views.

Deep pessimism is a lasting element of Silván's poetry:

I am always sad, at all times
dissatisfied
In great affliction
I ask for joy

Nothing worse can happen to me
For I have nothing more to lose

I am torn every way
I don't know what to do ...

Láni, represented by only a few works, is the best Slovak religious poet before Tranovský. Josef Minárik called him the most talented and the strongest personality in Slovak poetry. Each of Láni's ten songs is a sophisticated work of art. He was a Lutheran pastor in Mošovce, and he later came attached to the court of the rich Palatine Thurzo. His poetry is born of the tenor of the times – full of unsettling events, rumours of war, and Turkish incursions:

I am like to one on the roof
lonely sparrow,
bereft of consolation;
and like a friendless
handsome pelican
aged by his years;
friends stand afar,
and the enemies
burning with malice,
triumph.

A popular folk element often appears as well:

I am like the hermit in the mountains,
I am like the deer in the valley,
running along the dale,
searching for the living water;
Oh God, my God!

In a more secular vein is the poetry of Martin Rakovský (1535–79), who worked as a teacher in Prague and then as a principal in Louny. He was a member of the Hodějovský circle of Prague humanists, and later was named the Clerk of the Royal Hungarian Chamber in Bratislava. He wrote in Latin, composing elegies and the occasional poem dedicated to a group of illustrious and learned men, friends of his in Prague. His most important works were written in Slovakia. In Bratislava, he wrote a didactic, political poem in distich, dedicated to Emperor Maximilian II, *Libellus de partibus reipublicae et causis mutationum regnorum imperiumque* (A book about the social groups in the state and the causes of perturbations in kingdoms and empires, 1560). Considering the composition's dedication, it is quite bracing to see the author enumerate among the causes of disturbances the incompetence, sickness, laziness, wantonness, and tyranny of the ruler. A place of distinction is claimed by inequality:

> Most of the causes are generated by inequality, and therefore things turn upside down on its account, it is the originator of rebellions.
> Because it is inequality when in the administration of the citizens or distribution of advantages, there is no measure.
> If unequal people receive equally
> Though they are unequal, still they get the same gift.
> Because when the ruler is not able enough to rule the state, the administrator himself cannot have better manners.

Rakoský mentions mysterious, Platonic causes as well, and finally there are five theological causes: mysterious Divine Will, the faithlessness of people, the faithlessness and the idolatry of rulers, and punishment for the sins of nations and rulers. Nor does he not leave out social causes. He uses *exempla* to buttress his case. It is an astonishing work in its completeness and complexity, it is well organized and furnished with striking explanations. A companion to this volume is his next composition, also written for Maximilian II *De magistratu politico* (About the wordly powers, 1574), in which the ruler is defined as a person who is wielding power by the will of God. Among Rakovský's sources were classical authors such as Plato, Ovid, Plutarch, Hesiod, Homer, Seneca, and Cicero, as well as the Reformation authors Melanchton and Lauterbeck.

In a typical Renaissance genre were the epigrams of Ján Sambucus (1531–84), an outstanding polyhistor, philosopher, physician, and teacher who wrote in Latin. He is known for *Poemata quadem* (Some poems, 1555) and *Emblemata* (1564). One of his "emblems" is dedicated to his birthplace, Trnava ("Tirnaviae patriae meae arma" – The arms of my motherland Trnava):

> In Pannonian lands is a free city of glorious reputation known as Trnava, as our people call it.
> Belo, one of the wealthiest kings, surrounded it with walls and decorated it with battlements and towers.
> This sweet mother gave me birth, and also let me see the light of day, giving me the breath of life.
> In its emblem is a wheel guarded by divine messengers
> and it is safe under the protection of Christ.

But in our affairs nothing is certain without the Divine Will, the wheel will not stay put, it is in motion, as you know, against enemy armies and the terrible plague of Turks.
Courageously the city has defended itself until now.
It is rich in grain and wine, and has many merchants.
Strong in arms by rights, and known for its fear of God.
May Christ Himself protect it for many years in health and let the Turkish beast be dashed to pieces in honour!

As the above suggests, the Turkish threat was an ever-present concern. The reference to the desperate defence against the invaders comes from a highly artistic and anonymous historical poem, "Song about the Castle of Siget," which describes the siege of the Siget fortress by the Turkish host led by the Sultan Soliman II (1496–1566). There is a fine sense of gradation in the description of the siege; ever fresh, never repetitive, always engaging and surprising in its unusual detail. The heroic defenders were led by a Croatian captain, Nicholas Zrínsky (1508–66). Both Soliman and Zrínsky fell in the action. Fourteen Turkish assaults are described, each of them highly personified. During the twelfth attack, the defenders lose hope of victory and decide to fight to the last man in a desperate charge. The wives of many officers are in the fortress and they, understanding their predicament, ask to be beheaded, rather than let themselves fall into the Turkish hands. One of them asks for weapons and joins the men in the fourteenth assault. After killing a number of Turks, she is shot. When the Turks get inside the fortress, Zrínsky is dying. The Turks behead him, boil his head in vinegar, and impale it on a lance for exhibition.

Historical songs were a popular form, and there are several about the sacking by the Turks of the castles Modrý Kameň, Divín, Zvolen, and Somos. The oldest of this genre is a song about the Muráň Castle, written by Martin Bošňák, but it is unrelated to the Turkish menace. This song describes the defeat of a robber knight who, with his sons, operated from this castle 1522 to 1550). The fight was won by Count Nicholas of Salma, who led a force of Spanish mercenaries under the command of Ferdinand I.

Among the earliest Slovak Renaissance love poems is a beautiful, anonymous epic song in Slovakized Czech. This versified romance, entitled "A Song about Two Hungarian Gentlemen and the Daughter of the Turkish Emperor," also known as "Siládi and Hadmázi" (1560), was written by an *igric* as a "chronicle." Siládi and Hadmázi, the two gentlemen of the title are captured by the Turks and imprisoned in Constantinople. One day, as they are looking out of the prison window, one of them starts to sing a beautiful tune. The daughter of the Turkish sultan hears the song and comes to talk to Siládi. She falls in love and frees the men, giving each a golden sabre. Acting quickly, they choose the best horses, cut down the others, and make a dash for the Hungarian border. They are pursued, but manage to beat their pursuers off, while the sultan's daughter watches the action from behind bushes. They get home safely, but Hadmázi decides to challenge Siládi to a duel for the beautiful princess. She, in turn, begs them to cut her to pieces rather than fight for her, but they do fight, and Siládi cuts off Hadmazi's hand – his punishment for wanting the sultan's daughter while his own wife is waiting for him.

PROSE

The prose of this period branches out into a wide variety of genres. In religious prose, the Protestant cause is represented by a disproportionate number of texts. The Latin tradition of polemical speeches, funeral orations, dissertations, and diaries falls outside the framework of fiction, but was important in building a repertoire of literary expression both in Latin and in Slovakized Czech. Travelogues are a common form (one example is a description by Jan Dernschwan, from Banská Bystrica, of his trip to Constantinople in 1553). Philosophy, history, law, linguistics, literary theory – all find their authors in this age.

Of particular interest are two authors: Ján Jessenius (1566–1621) and Vavrinec Benedikt Nedožerský (1555–1615), also known as Nedozerinus or Benedicti. Jessenius, a rector of Charles University in Prague, became famous for performing the first autopsy in Bohemia. He was executed in 1621, after the defeat of the Czech cause at the Battle of the White Mountain, which brought in the Hapsburg rule that lasted until 1918. Apart from medicine, he wrote on philosophy and was a follower of neo-Platonist ideas (*Zoroaster*, 1593). He wrote occasional orations, including one praising Mathias II (1609) and one mourning his friend Tycho de Brahe (1601). Jessenius is one of the few Slovaks who exercised great influence due to his early success outside Slovakia, and he is honoured in the country as a great scientist, philosopher, and man of letters.

Nedožerský was a professor of mathematics and classical philology (an unthinkable combination today), and dean and pro-rector of the faculty of arts at Charles University (1604–15). His early work comprises some eighty highly polished occasional poems in Latin. In 1603, he published *Grammaticae Bohemicae libri duo* (Two books of Czech grammar), nine years in the preparation. It was the first systematic grammar of the Czech language, beginning a trend that lasted for centuries – with their nationhood lost, Slovaks would make their contributions for the benefit of other nations. Nedožerský's grammar had a great influence in the early nineteenth century, the modern Czech literary language was standardized.

Slovak Protestants used the biblical Czech, *bibličtina* (from the *Kralice Bible*, 1594), as their church language, and so codifying its grammar must have seemed a logical step. After all, there was a need that had to be addressed: the Slovakizing tendency of ordinary parishioners, for whom Czech was a foreign language despite its resemblance to Slovak. Nevertheless, Nedožerský is not trying to turn Slovaks into Czechs at all. His point is different:

> It seems to me that I have to say a word to my Slovak compatriots, who are so careless in the cultivation of their language – so much so that some of them (and I speak from experience) are boasting not only that they do not read any Czech books, but that they do not have a single one in their libraries. And so it happens that when they have to speak about something in their own language, they have to speak half in Latin ... I am not forcing them to speak Czech but to exercise and cultivate their own language, especially since they have so many schools not only in the cities and towns, but also in the villages.

Schools were of great interest to Nedožerský as he made clear in a rather long poem in Latin hexameters, *Penitioris scholae structura* (Structure of the lower schools, 1607), in which he suggested various reforms to the school system.

The case of Nedožerský provides ample argument for the possibly controversial inclusion in histories of Slovak literature of authors writing in a different language. Nodožerský's point of view in the above quotation unambiguously shows that he saw himself as a Slovak author, mindful of the fact that he was writing in Czech. He encouraged Slovaks to cultivate their own language, suggesting that it was preferable to use Czech, rather than Latin, for communication.

DRAMA

The polarization of religious life during the Renaissance led to a similar polarization in educational institutions. Protestant schools, following foreign models, organized performances of Latin school plays, which diminished the role of mysteries and Passion-plays. Although they were at first performed in Lutheran schools (in Banská Bystrica, Banská Štiavnica, Bardcjov, Kežmarok, and elsewhere), they could soon be seen in the Catholic schools as well (in Trnava, Kláštor pod Znievom, Humenné, Bratislava, Košice, Spišská Kapitula, Brezno, Prešov, and elsewhere).

While the educational aim predominated, there were other reasons for performing these plays. They provided a test of students' Latin and their ability to perform in public, but, because of their religious basis (they were mostly taken from the Old Testament), they had a wider educational and propaganda purpose, whether pro- or anti-Reformation.

Some plays were written in Latin by Andrej Rochotský (*Gedeon*, 1603), but there were also plays in Czech by the Slovak playwrights Pavel Kyrmezer and Juraj Tesák-Mošovský. Kyrmezer (d. 1589) is the most significant dramatic author in Slovak and Czech of this period. He wrote three plays: *Komédia česká o bohatci a lazarovi* (Czech comedy about Lazarus and the rich man, 1566), *Komédia nová o vdově* (New comedy about the widow, 1573), and *Komédia o Tobiášovi* (A comedy about Tobias, 1581). Of these, *Komédia nova o vdově* is the best. Though he had a German model in a play by Leonhard Culmann, Kyrmezer managed to add to the biblical content of the story – Rachel who cannot pay her debt and her miraculous deliverance by a prophet – some contemporary elements that turn the play into a powerful and timely statement. He achieved this partly through his masterful use of spoken language and his very realistic characters, who ingratiate themselves to the audience by quoting well-known proverbs and locutions. Tesák-Mošovský (1545–1617) wrote a verse drama, *Komédie z knihy Zákona božího, jenž slove Ruth, sebraná* (A comedy from the testament of God, called Ruth, 1604), a loose dramatization of the biblical story of Noami and Ruth.

In Trnava, the Jesuit schools in addition to staging stories taken from ancient sources, began to take an interest in recent history, and performed a play about St Adalbert and Boleslav II, in 1641.

FOLK LITERATURE

In the fifteenth century, a process of differentiation was under way in folk literature. While traditional folk literature, with its loose connection to the seasonal and Christian calendars and its rituals, continued as before, the lyric song devolved into a number of separate genres, such as family, military, pastoral, humorous, love, and work songs (the *trávnice* – "grass songs"), and lullabyes. A separate category developing in this age was the ballad, which would play a larger role in nineteenth-century romantic literature. Renaissance ballads told dramatic, tragic stories connected to the many wars of the period. There were also military and robbers' ballads, and ballads of family tragedies, adultery, and even murders, reminiscent of romances.

The history of the period is particularly present in the ballads about King Mathias, in the fifteenth century, and the resistance to the Turkish invasions, in the sixteenth and seventeenth centuries. These are not grand descriptions of major battles, but portraits of family tragedies occasioned by the Turkish wars. To these were added the powerful genre of recruiting songs, in which people sang of the hunt for human cannon fodder, the attempts of mothers to hide their sons, and attempts to escape a draft that would almost certainly result in death. The sorrow of those who did not escape their fate as soldiers is also told in these songs. Such favourites as "Dobrú noc má milá, dobrú noc" (Good night, my dear, good night) and "Žalo dievča, žalo trávu" (The girl who cut the grass) come from the end of the fifteenth century.

JURAJ TRANOVSKÝ (1592–1637)

Tranovský is the best known of all Slovak hymn writers. Born in Silesia, he became a Lutheran pastor in Liptovský Svätý Mikuláš. His place in history is due to the publication in Levoča of a collection of 414 of his songs called the *Cithara Sanctorum* (1636). Almost immediately, it became the most popular and widely used hymn-book not only in Slovakia, but also in Bohemia and Moravia, among Czech groups in Lusatia, and even among Polish groups in Silesia, where it was used until 1865. Some of the songs were taken from the Czech author Steyr's hymnbook, but some ninety are ascribed to Tranovský. They are predominantly church songs in the sense that they fulfil a catechetical function by explaining the Immaculate Conception, the divinity of Christ, Original Sin, salvation through the Blood of Christ, and other doctrines. Tranovský was also influenced by Eliáš Láni; his main theme is the great struggle with the devil, who can be overcome by a religious song. About forty songs are from the Slovak, others are translations from Latin (eight) or German (sixty), and the rest are Czech.

Perhaps it is difficult to see now how this hymn-book could have served as the source for raising national consciousness, as well as being a pioneering work of Slovak music, but this only underscores the paucity of sources that could free educted Slovaks from their dependency on the culture of their political masters. Thus, even this hymn-book, which went through more than 150 editions, could serve such a function. The Catholic hymn-book by Benedikt Szőllősi (1609–56), *Cantus Catholici. Písně catholické latinské i slovenské* (Catholic songs in Latin and Slovak, 1655), shares more than one hundred songs with Tranovský's *Cithara Sanctorum.*

Besides this work's ostensible purpose, it may have contained another, hidden purpose. Perhaps it assisted in the secret, steady formation of a national consciousness at a time when many educated people could find very little in their literature upon which their emerging awareness could feed. This was very different from the situation that had existed just thirty years before, when Nedožerský addressed his critical words to Slovaks.

Thus, the period of the literary Renaissance bore the seed of the triumphant national revival that would bear fruit in the late eighteenth and first half of the nineteenth centuries. The medieval Slovak, who thought himself as a member of God's family, a member of his own family, then perhaps a member of his clan, town, village, or region, but never as a member of a *nation*, was no more. Not that a national consciousness stepped into the void immediately, it was a lengthy process, lasting over two hundred years, at the beginning of which a strong bond was forged between the individual and his denomination in the times of the Reformation and Counter-Reformation. Then – partly because of the loss of the Czech cause in 1620 – the national element stepped in. Nor was the defeat at White Mountain in 1620 a clear-cut *national* battle. It was a religious, "confessional" conflict, and the Czechs, as some modern Czech historians believe, would have fared worse *nationally* had "their" cause proved victorious in the battle, for they might have been swallowed by the strong tide of militant Prussian German nationalism and assimilated completely. From that sad fate, they had to be rescued by the hated Hapsburgs. It was a paradox, for in their misfortune they actually saved their nation and, through the many exiles in Slovakia (for many Czechs preferred to live in the kingdom of Hungary), supported the formation of the same national consciousness in their Protestant Slovak brethren. The interesting career of Jakub Jakobeus bears this out.

Jakobeus (1591–1645) was from Kutná Hora, in Bohemia, and the author of *Gentis Slavonicae lacrumae, suspiria et vota* (Tears, sighs, and requests of the Slovak nation, 1642). While he clearly understood the Slovak nation in the ethnic sense, the sharp denominational differences of the period led him to identify as Slovaks only those of Lutheran confession, although his key figure, the "Slovak Mother," remained a symbol of the entire nation. And so, while we have a Slovak who wrote a Czech grammar, we also have a Czech who wrote a passionate panegyric to the Slovak nation. Both are evidence of the real presence of something new – a nascent national consciousness.

3 Baroque (1636–1780)

The Baroque literature written in Slovakia between 1650 and 1780 was the product of a contradictory age in at least two senses. First, in this period the contradiction observable in the Renaissance deepened even further. If the Renaissance meant a certain freedom from religious strictures, the Baroque period, despite various movements to the contrary, continued further in this direction. Second, the Baroque age was a reaction to the unrealized promise of the Renaissance. Instead of a more rational and peaceful life, there was more religious strife; in Slovakia, Turkish attacks continued until 1687. As well, there were numerous anti-Hapsburg rebellions among the Hungarian nobility, and, fairly or not, Slovakia was implicated. The still unsettled religious division, which, during the reign of Leopold I, led to harsh repression and persecution of Protestants, persisted. Finally, perhaps because of the prolonged and costly period of military activity, there was an economic crisis near the end of the seventeenth century.

All of these factors contributed to a feeling of malaise and a sense of disappointment with the promise so seductively offered by the Renaissance credo of man as the measure of all things. If man himself was in need of help, where could he turn but back to God? The real need for transcendence may not be explained by a catalogue of evils, but irrespective of this need, the unravelling of history, an irresistible and entropic process, meant that any return to orthodoxy was ineffectual in bringing about a real change in the general religious, social, and political course of events.

One sign of this apparently inexorable development was a definite division between sacred and profane literature, a process that had begun during the Renaissance. By the end of the Baroque period, another swing of the pendulum would bring the Enlightenment, as it was ironically called. If we take the much-maligned Middle Ages as the point of departure, the Baroque deepened the divisions and further shattered the unity that had existed during the medieval period, for the inevitable had happened in the Protestant world: further divisions, further atomization. Simultaneously, the Counter-Reformation made advances on the territories lost to the Protestants. Whatever the effort and suffering involved, the division was not healed but exacerbated by the use of violence against Protestants.

The modern age looks with horror at the religious wars, despite a recrudescence of this phenomenon in the latter half of the twentieth century. It is rarely realized that participants in these wars have often used the ultimate justification, "If it is not worthwhile to fight for God, what is worthwhile to fight for? Real estate? Money?"

The last chapter of interreligious intolerance in Slovakia was acted out during the Baroque era, in which, despite everything, lasting spiritual values were added to the treasury of Slovak literature. The list of authors grew in this period, and so did the list of scholars and teachers; a firm basis was being established for the next age to unleash a powerful revival of national aspirations, accompanied by a surge of creativity in literature.

The massive structures, adorned with excessive ornamentation, so typical of the Baroque aesthetic are also visible in the literature of this age. A counterpoint to this solidity is a contradictory idea expressed as a frequent literary *topos*: *vanitas vanitatum*, the ultimate vanity of all human effort.

POETRY

In addition to religious poetry, already firmly established as a genre, secular poetry appears more frequently during the Baroque period. In Protestant poetry, a major role was played by a new edition (1674) of Tranovský's *Cithara sanctorum*, which featured a promising number of Slovak songs. Among the important Slovak songwriters included were Gašpar Motešický (1651–89), Ján Kromholc (d. 1683), Adam Plintovič and Jeremiáš Lednický (between 1633 and 1706), Juraj Zábojník (1608–72), and, particularly, Daniel Sinapius-Horčička, Sr (1640–88), who wrote emotionally charged and nostalgic songs, expressing the essential feelings of Baroque man.

From the point of view of language, Catholic poetry, particularly that in songs, made an effort to get closer to the people and their language. It is in Catholic song that we see a change from the heretofore not very Slovakized Czech to greater use of Slovakisms, and, by the end of the period, we can properly speak of Slovak with Bohemisms – that is, Bohemized Slovak, rather than Slovakized Czech.

There may have been some religious-political motives behind this movement in the sense that the Counter-Reformation naturally tried to attract the attention of the people. On the other hand, what with the appearance of Czech grammars and better-educated Protestant laymen, the continuing use of biblical Czech for Protestant services acted as a conservative force against linguistic evolution: there was little incentive to change, nor could change have been effected simply, since it would be connected with matters of church policy.

In the middle of the seventeenth century, the Catholic answer to Tranovský appeared in Benedikt Szőllősi's (1609–56) *Cantus catholici, Písně katholické latinské i slovenské* (Catholic songs Latin and Slovak, 1655, 1700). Szőllősi was a Jesuit priest, and his preface, written in Latin, is an interesting document. It spells out Slovak national and patriotic feelings, going so far as to mention the tradition of saints Cyril and Methodius and the glorious Slovak past. However, the more than forty songs with a Slovak background (some of which date from the second half of the sixteenth century) are outnumbered by the more than one hundred and eighty Czech songs. As mentioned, *Cantus Catholici* shares about one hundred songs with the *Cithara sanctorum.* The Baroque sensibility is represented in mystical love poetry with Marian and Jesus themes. The following verses are typical of Slovak religious Baroque poetry:

And sometimes I speak to myself as if to a man:
If I could fly freely like a dove,
I would fly as far as I could
to the lonely forests,
and there I would spend my life
and live out this age.

A very large number of songs have a nativity theme, and it is here that the Baroque tradition of Baby Jesus is introduced in a popular manner reminiscent of Christmas carols.

A major theme of the historical epic was the Turkish wars. A special place in this literature belongs to Štefan Pilárik, Sr (1615–93), and his poem *Sors Pilarikiana – Los Pilárika Štěpána* (Pilárik's fate, 1666), an autobiographical account of Pilárik's experiences as a prisoner of the Turks, who captured him in 1663, as he was walking to Senica to take up his post as pastor. At this point, Pilárik interrupts the dramatic account to make a biblical digression on the arrest of Jesus. This, of course, is not simply literary technique – it is the way that a Christian pastor would think, given the circumstances – but it is used throughout the epic poem. Each indignity, each example of suffering, immediately evokes a biblical counterpart that not only adds meaning to Pilárik's suffering, but makes it easier for him to survive. The poem provides a horrifying account of the seemingly irrational bestiality of the Turks, who were behaving abominably to the women. After Pilárik is stripped of his habit, he is thrown a nondescript tunic and socks, which have to suffice in the rainy, cool night. The Turks tried to sell some of their prisoners, and they let Pilárik know that if he is not sold, he will be beheaded. Eventually, a Turk decides to sell Pilárik to a Wallachian (Rumanian) leader of a detachment called Vulkuli. Since the Turk does not get as much as he wants for Pilárik, he beats him up in frustration. Pilárik feels better in the Wallachian camp. His fellow prisoners are Christians, and suddenly, after fighting with the Catholics for so long, Pilárik finds that he has, after all, more in common with his fellow Catholic prisoners than with the Turks:

> We, who could not stand
> each other in happiness, joined in the misfortune
> not in the religion
> but in a common comradeship

Pilárik's conversations with a Jesuit priest named Linga are among the most interesting passages of the poem.

Pilárik is then bought to become a teacher for his new master's children, whom he is to instruct in the literary arts. But another Wallachian helps him to escape, and so he crosses the Danube to Komárno with Father Linga. Here, Pilárik has the good fortune to meet the Croatian hero Zrínsky, who later dies defending the Siget fortress. Finally, Pilárik arrives home, where his children hardly recognize him.

Social criticism and satire can be found in the poetry of Peter Benický (1603–64). He wrote in Hungarian and in Slovak – *Slovenské verše* (Slovak verses, 1652) – but these poems were not published until 1873. As a nobleman, Benický glorified personal freedom, but he also demonstrated the responsibility that went with his status by displaying his sympathy with the peasants. While he satirized laziness and praised work, he mercilessly ridiculed the noblemen, especially the cowardly ones. His manner of expression showed the excess typical of any Baroque author, but it is tempered by its wealth of folk sayings, proverbs, and everyday locutions.

Catholic Baroque poetry at its best is represented by Ján Abrahámffy's *Knížka modliteb nábožných* (The book of religious prayers, 1693). This is a collection of prose and versified prayers inspired by the horrors of the times (Turkish wars, rebellions) and imbued with deep Franciscan religiosity and mysticism.

Konštantín Halapi's (1698–1752) moralizing and didactic secular poetry, written in Latin epigrams of astonishing variety and inventiveness, was collected in *Epigrammatum moralium, aenigmatum ac tumulorum libri VII* (Seven books of moral epigrams, riddles, and funeral inscriptions, 1745). With wit, humour, irony, and satire the author attacks a variety of topics based on biblical and historical themes. He is critical of his times, which he calls *Aetas ferrea et plumbea*, the Age of Iron and Lead. There are sharp attacks on some of the "negative" characteristics of women (an old *topos*), but unquestionably the most unusual and curious part of the collection comprises Halapi's riddles:

I am a mouth and have a great number of teeth,
I have a disdain for food and I never hunger
Bald heads don't know me, but I see the hairy ones often
At the back of his head my master carries me

(*Pecten* – Comb)

His funeral inscriptions betray real gallows humour:

Breezes are fanning me, the rain washes away the dark spots,
I was a thieving raven, and then I became a swan.
My tongue laughs from my open mouth at those who laugh at me:
"I'll step down from my throne, if anyone will take it."

The love lyric of the period has a special genre called *à la mode*, suggesting its origin in France, where this gallant, even "precious" type of poetry had been cultivated since the seventeenth century. In the Slovak love lyric, the genre stresses love as a tormenting pain and seems rather affected due to its use of foreign words. It is the poetry of the lower nobility and townfolk, and the diction is very close to that of spoken Slovak:

Don't torment me, traitorous Venus,
don't torment my heart,
for I can't bear any more
your false ways.
You always hurt
and never heal,
you take away my heart
and hide yours away,
tormenting mine, you won't let yours be tormented

A real jewel of love poetry is Štefan Ferdinand Selecký's versified composition *Obraz panej krásnej perem malovaný, která ma v Trnave svoje prebývaní* (The picture of a beautiful lady of Trnava drawn with pen, 1701). In this composition of 332 verses, divided into three cantos, Selecký merges the image of the Beautiful Lady with the image of Trnava University and that of Science. The allegory, however, is never obvious or forcefully pressed, and the suspense born of this ambiguity heightens the artistic tension of this remarkable work.

At the end of the Baroque period, Catholic religious poetry finally matched the heretofore more productive Protestant poetry. Not all Catholic poetry was published. Particularly noteworthy are the Franciscan hymn-books, with their emphasis on Christmas hymns and carols. Edmund Pascha (1714–72) and Juraj Bajan (1721–92) are two prominent authors of this genre. Pascha's *Harmonia pastoralis – Prosae pastorali* (Pastoral harmony – pastoral songs, 1770) is a Latin mass for Christmas with Slovak folk carols and shepherds' songs *(pastoralia)*, including "Do lesa, do hory valasi" ("Go to the woods, to the mountains, shepherds"). All of them skilfully use a backdrop with which the believers are very familiar: the mountains and shepherds are not Palestinian, but recognizably Slovak.

Hugolín Gavlovič (1712–87)

A Franciscan since 1733, the Slovak-educated Hugolín Gavlovič, a native of Silesia, wrote the greatest poem of the Baroque age, *Valaská škola mravuv stodola* (Shepherds' school as a treasury of morals, 1755), published only in 1830–31 but achieving its due recognition in recent times, as can be seen the remarkable study of this work by a leading American Slovakist, Fr Gerald Sabo, SJ.

In the tradition of some Renaissance and Baroque works that are encyclopaedic in breadth, *Valaská škola* is designed and built like a grand basilica. It is a structurally perfect arrangement of 1,298 poems arranged into twenty-one cantos, which Gavlovič calls "shepherd's notes." These notes use as a model a biblical theme, often applied to the life of the shepherds, and they are followed by fifty-nine independent poems called "concepts." After the twenty-one cantos is an "addendum" of another fifty-nine poems. The work was written in Bohemized Slovak.

True to the Baroque spirit, Gavlovič meditates on vanity; criticizes superstition, wars, drunkenness, bribery, and other evils; and promotes love of homeland, tradition, and literature, while expressing a great admiration for the poor. He is very censorious toward the nobles and masters, whose moral life he finds wanting. His work reveals a sense of stubborn independence born of deep meditation and holiness.

There is a biographical explanation for Gavlovič's admiration of simple peasants. He suffered from a disease of the lungs. For years, he spent the winter in the Franciscan monastery in Pruské and, after 1745, his summers on a *salash* – a high mountain chalet belonging to Slovak shepherds. Some of his oft-quoted verses express clearly his preference for the "lowly":

> As the sinner with the just man, a holy man with a dog,
> so is for the poor of this world the rich man.
> Lions seek their wherewithal in the desert
> while the rich feast on the poor.

Further on, he writes,

> The robbers steal in the mountains, the nobles in the villages.
> They are worse than the robbers, for the world doesn't stop them.
> This master robs his peasants by taking more bread
> than he needs according to justice.
> Without warning, he robs them till they cry out to heaven,
> They have to suffer for, except for God, they have no hope.
> Don't say you can do with your peasant what you want,
> you have to follow God's commandments in all things!

The last stern warning suggests a bracing, even overwhelmingly dry and studious tone, but Gavlovič successfully avoids this by interpolating some gems of wisdom in the form of folk poetry, such as *"Hovadá provázek, slovo ľudí váže"* (Beasts by a string, people by a word are drawn).

Each poem has a tripartite structure: prologue, moral, epilogue. The prologue is the title or motto of the given poem. The verse consists of fourteen syllables divided by a caesura into eight and six. "You have to say all eight with one breath, then you are left with six,"

Gavlovič writes, advising his readers to put a melody to his verses, and indeed they are very melodious.

The uniqueness of Gavlovič's work may derive from the contrast between his solid education (the Bible, the Church Fathers, and the classics – Seneca, Aristotle, Ovid, Plautus, Pliny, Thomas à Kempis, Erasmus) and the natural wisdom he found at the *salash.* Here is one representative example of this unusual mixture: when Cain kills his brother, Abel, Gavlovič writes, "*Vycedil krev zlostní sedlák z valacha prvního*" (An angry peasant spilled the blood of the first shepherd). Although the rough dialectal Slovak is lost in the translation, even in English one can see the comical contrast between the elevated style of the Bible and the rough peasant-like style. But there is no humour here at the expense of the faith; Gavlovič is theologically sound. It is as if the long time he spent in the *salash* confirmed in him the religion of the Bible by a transmutation of the textual wisdom and its incarnation in the shepherds he observed.

Gavlovič's discovery that the pastoral setting of Palestine could be superimposed on the *salash* is the key to understanding his work. He not only humanizes eternal wisdom, but he dignifies the simple shepherd, quite naturally taking his side, and cannot see the local nobles as anything but parasites. One is left to wonder if this clear and unambiguous attitude was not the reason for the delay in publication of this learned Franciscan's great work.

Also of interest is Gavlovič's ethical system. His concept of ethics (which he amusingly calls *polícia* – police) is divided into three types: "Christian," "civil," and "secular." The person with the first set of ethics aims for the glory of God and has a good conscience and good morals. The person with the second set aims for the peace and prosperity of his neighbour and has a good conscience, but bad morals. He with the last set aims for self-praise, and has both a bad conscience and bad morals.

Despite the strong moral charge that issues from each of Gavlovič's poems, the cumulative effect of the whole suggests a different result than the moral one, as Krčméry has noted, which can be summarized by Gavlovič's belief that "there is no greater wealth than literature." Inded, it is his love of literature that comes through most clearly – not only in his wealth of allusions and background of classical literature, but in his love of creating literature, playing with words, building an awesome structure, and using the most unusual material – the speech of the simple, uneducated peasants, who are made to speak, through the miracle of literature, like Pliny, or like Moses.

Like many works of literary art encyclopaedic in scope, *Valaská škola* is not to be read continuously. That would be impossible, for the text is too demanding, too thick with meaning. It is meant to be savoured, but in small doses.

Gavlovič wrote other major works: *Škola kresťanská* (Christian school, 1758), *Škola duchovní* (Spiritual school, 1777), *Kamen pomoci* (The stone of help, 1779), *Kniha marnosti sveta* (The book of the vanity of the world, 1780), and *Peťsto naučení o dobrých mravoch* (Five Hundred lessons about good manners), all of them unpublished.

Jánošík

A separate chapter would be needed to explore fully the Jánošík myth, or legend. Despite his many detractors among critics and historians, the myth bears all the signs of longevity and vitality. Juraj Jánošík, a thief – or, rather, a brigand – was executed by hanging on a hook in 1713. His last words were, "Now that you have roasted me, you will have to eat me!" And with these words Jánošík is said to have jumped on the hook himself, spurning the chance of an imperial pardon and army service instead of execution. Or so says the legend. There is in Slovak poetry of the Baroque period an entire corpus of "Jánošík poems," as well as an early-eighteenth-century "Song of Jánošík," which celebrates robbery of the Jánošík kind: taking from the rich in order to help the poor, in Robin Hood fashion.

Folk poetry has endowed Jánošík with almost supernatural powers. He has unusual abilities, and magic is always around him. It is as if the last vestiges of pagan superstition found refuge with him. His belt was magical; when he took it off, he was captured. Or he was caught because an evil old woman threw a bowlful of dry peas in his way as he tried to escape from the gendarmes.

Transformations also occurred in the topography of Jánošík's exploits. The headquarters where he kept his fire burning is Kráľová Hoľa, now a nearly mystical site. In fact, it does seem to be the heart of Slovakia; both the Hron and the Hornád, important rivers, issue from it and, standing at the top of the round hill, one can see mountain ranges all around and can peer into the valleys. But Kráľová Hoľa has been endowed with a special cachet, which it did not have before Jánošík. A frustrated passion for justice (which made Gavlovič's blood boil, as he inveighed against injustices) made him an avenging angel. This is why it is important that he started his career as a seminarian: he was no savage, he knew his God, but the people needed his help ...

Jánošík always outsmarted his enemies. Even in death he was magnificent. Many people appreciate his pride and his disdain for death. His death, too, had a strange aftermath, producing a feeling of sadness mixed with pride and a trace of belief that he was not really dead, or that he had left behind some talisman (perhaps even a hidden treasure, which many have tried to find; something that each child in the Upper Hron region dreams of even today) …

PROSE

This is the age of further and steady improvements in secular prose, although religious prose is still predominant, due to the need to produce polemical religious tracts to justify continuing religious division and controversy. Apart from such polemics, there was a need to supply the new readership with new catechisms and prayer-books. One of the authors of the latter was Daniel Sinapius-Horčička, Sr.

To simplify matters somewhat, the confessional division led to two distinct literary orientations. The Protestant cause was represented by theological dissertations – almost none of them original, but rehashes of established arguments and sources. The Catholic authors wrote funeral orations, a surprisingly popular genre at the time, and sermons.

The persecution of the Protestants (1672–74), which was of a mercifully short duration, led to a tremendous outpouring of memoirs relating their sufferings. Mostly by pastors who refused to switch sides. Closely linked to this group of works is another set of memoirs, which also originated in persecution and exile, but that perpetrated by the Turks. Štefan Pilárik penned a prose account entitled *Turcico-Tartarica crudelitas, das ist: Derer Turcken und Tartarn Grausamkeit* (Turkish-Tatar cruelty, that is: the cruelty of the Turks and Tatars, 1684). On a similar topic is Samuel Chalúpka, Sr's *Vandrovka aneb Putování prežalostné Roziny Puchalky, Samuele Chalúpky manželky* (The wanderings and peregrinations of the sorrowful Rozina Puchalka, the wife of Samuel Chalúpka, 1663), describing the fate of his wife, who was captured by the Turks and taken to Wallachia (Romania), from where she managed to return. Rather than a factual, documentary account of his imprisonment by the Turks free of the strictures that the poetic form imposed on him in his previous work, *Sors Pilarikiana*, Pilárik used his experiences as a point of departure for a rather fictionalized story. While the central facts remain the same, Pilárik uses them as an opportunity to meditate upon the role of Divine intervention in the affairs of men.

The persecution of the Protestants was also the topic of Joachim Kalinka's (1601–78) *Diarium* (Diary, 1671–72), in which he describes his incarceration in Pressburg (Bratislava) in 1671–72. Kalinka's work, like Pilárik's, shows evidence of a considerable effort to give a literary shape to an otherwise straightforward document. Ján Simonides

(1648–1708), similarly persecuted, produced a very interesting and voluminous text in Latin, *Incarceratio, liberatio et peregrinatio* (Imprisonment, liberation, and pilgrimage, 1676), which provides an excellent memoir (and travelogue) of the Slovak Baroque.

Incarceratio begins with Simonides's imprisonment and trial in 1674 in Bratislava, continues with his incarceration in Leopoldov prison and in Naples via Slovakia, Moravia, Austria, Slovenia, the Adriatic Sea, and Italy. At this point the author manages to escape, but he is again imprisoned and then rescued by a German merchant. After his liberation, Simonides and his friend Masník (another author of memoirs) tour the great Italian cities and return home via Switzerland and Germany. Other sections are devoted to Naples, Rome, and Venice. In Rome, Simonides visits the ancient ruins and provides a detailed description of the Basilica of St Peter.

Writing of his sea voyage, Simonides makes numerous digressions, which, somehow, do not interrupt the narrative of his travels. This is yet another memoir in which the author digests and recasts his material in what he considers to be a "literary" manner: lyricism and passion rescue this type of writing from being a mere catalogue of places and events. But there are passages where rough diamonds shine even in the middle of the night, as in his description of a storm on the Adriatic Sea:

> But on the sixteenth of April (the third day of Easter), in the
> evening and all night long, a mighty storm rolled over the
> ship, so that it sounded like it was splitting open. Yes,
> the
> waves were covering the deck, which otherwise stood nine
> yards above the water. And when the rocking ship began to
> flood, they broke the deck open, letting the water fall on
> our
> heads, so that it would provide the ship with ballast
> and save the top part. Then they pumped the water out.
> Even the sailors were losing hope that they
> would be
> saved. They could cast anchor only when the danger was
> the greatest. The ship was turning this way and that:
> it seemed upside down. That is why the soldiers said that
> the
> storm came because of the presence of heretics
> of the
> worst Godless kind. They were ready to throw us into the sea
> and were only waiting for the officers' go-ahead. Stormy

bouncing,
cries, in such a narrow place (all the
soldiers
were sent down and they beat us into the corner, so that we
were on top of each other) it became so
hot that we
sweated as in a furnace. And many had sea-sickness and were
throwing up
(pardon the expression). Many were so weak that they
seemed to be wrestling with death. In these horrible
sufferings,
following prayers and entreaties with sighs, the sun came up.

Simonides was among the outstanding scholars of his time, and in his writings (for example, his introduction to *Vysvětlení křesťanského učení,* [An explanation of Christian teaching, 1704]), he deliberately Slovakized the Czech language.

Similarly noteworthy is Juraj Láni's (1646–1701) German diary of his sufferings and peregrinations, *Kurze und wahrhafte historische Erzählung* (Short and truthful historical account, 1676). It is an excellent companion volume to Simonides, giving a more rounded picture of the times. Láni emphasizes his personal experiences, rather than his travels; particularly powerful are his descriptions of witch-burning.

The defence of the Slovak language, the nation, and Slavdom became more outspoken, as Daniel Sinapius Horčička, Sr's preface to his collection of proverbs *Neo-forum Latino-Slavonicum* (New Latin-Slovak treasury, 1678) demonstrates. Among his justifications for the Slovak nation are its ancient origin, settlement on vast territories in Hungary, the hospitality and hard work of its people, and, above all, its excellent language. More forcefully than Jakobeus, Horčička, Sr, attacks Slovaks who have a condescending attitude toward their own language and prefer Latin. This is an important point. It was not until some hundred and fifty years later, in the mid-nineteenth century, that Hungarian displaced Latin as the language forced on Slovaks.

Horčička, Sr, was also a pioneer in another sense. He translated some five hundred proverbs into Slovak, proving that this language was capable of the kind of expression that was thought possible only in Latin. Latin expressions, proverbs, and sayings have not disappeared from the vocabulary of Slovak intellectuals even today (after the Communist take-over, in 1948, Latin was dropped from the secondary-school curriculum, but it was reinstated after 1968). How much more common must the desire have been to impress one's peers with one's education when access to schooling was more limited than it is today?

Translators have always been esteemed in Slovakia, for they were (and are) thought of not only as transmitters and interpreters of foreign texts, but also as re- or co-discoverers of the potential of the Slovak language. Writers like Horčička, Sr, and his successors demonstrated this. Thus it was, and is, a rare writer of excellence in Slovakia who is not a published translator as well.

The type of memoir displaying the kind of sophistication and learning that has not dated is demonstrated by Daniel Krman, Jr's (1663–1740) Latin-Slovak memoirs, particularly his travel diary, *Itinerarium*, based on his journey to visit the Swedish king, Charles XII, then engaged in a decisive battle against his nemesis, the Russian emperor, Peter the Great. Krman's intention was to appeal to the Swedish king as a protector of Slovak Protestants, but this intention is buried under an avalanche of dramatic action. Krman has taken his embassy to the Swedish king at the most inconvenient time imaginable, and he pays for this bad timing.

Itinerarium contains detailed observations of an ethnographic character. Krman's journey took him to places then not usually seen by Slovaks: Poland, Lithuania, Prussia, Byelorussia, the Ukraine, and Moldavia. He makes valuable and very objective notes on the Ukrainians, Russians, Turks, Tatars, and Kalmyks, reserving most of his sympathy, not surprisingly, for the Swedes. However, this does not prevent him from describing the marauding tactics of the Swedish army in Lithuania. Of great historical import are his descriptions of the main actors in the great drama that was unfolding: Francis II, Rákoczi, Peter the Great, Mazeppa, and Charles XII.

Krman had a great gift for epic momentum, and the disaster of Charles XII's expedition – which was due as much to Peter the Great's cunning as to the impossibility of fighting the Russian terrain and the cold (as Napoleon and Hitler were also to find out) – shows this to advantage. Most dramatic is the author's escape following the defeat of the Swedes, with the enemy in pursuit. Here, the most engaging feature of Krman's account is his brilliant description of the breakdown of perhaps the world's best military machine at the time, led by a talented leader – some say genius – of military tactics and strategy. His accounts of chaotic forced marches in vicious cold and crossings of the river Dnieper have the immediacy and lack of bias of good reporting. Krman also wrote an encomium of the Slovak language, a grammar of Czech, and other works.

In contrast to Krman's approach to the memoir is the work of Samuel Hruškovič (1694–1748), *Vita Samuelis Hruskowitz* (The life of Samuel Hruškovič, 1719–20). This memoir, written in Latin, covers the author's life up to 1720, revealing a sensitive and pious soul whose vicissitudes, such as a miserable childhood and student years lived on the edge of starvation, lead him to a transcendental, almost mystical view of life. He is a sincere writer who manages, at times, to communicate an almost uncanny mood of intimacy to the reader. (Compare Rousseau's celebrated *Confessions*, with its irksome insincerity peppered with frequent declarations of frankness and truthfulness.) Hruškovič makes no declarations, but we sense the palpable truth of his words.

This was the age of encyclopaedists, among them Martin Szentivanyi (1633–1705). His *Curiosiora et selectiora variarum scientiarum miscellanea* (Curious and selected miscellanea from various sciences, 1689–1702) includes information culled from physics, astronomy, mathematics, geology, geography, history, medicine, law, philosophy, politics, and theology. But the most outstanding scientist of his age was Matej Bel (1684–1749).

Today, one can only wonder at the universalism of the great scientists of the Baroque period. They believed that the human intellect can and must absorb, digest, and apply the sum total of all knowledge. Modern man, rightly, if dimly, knowing himself to be unequal to this task, finds it difficult – if not impossible – to understand a man like Bel. Yet he found it possible to write, with as much authority as was possible at the time, on Hungarian culture (and here we must distinguish between "Hungarian," which refers to matters concerning the *multinational* state of the kingdom of Hungary, and "Magyar," which refers only to the Magyar component of the state and is not used pejoratively), history, linguistics, literature, ethnography, geography, economy, and natural science. He also wrote in a variety of languages: Latin, German, Hungarian, and Czech.

Bel was a pioneer of modern scientific method. He made use of a wide network of collaborators, drew on library and archival resources, and always drew up a rational plan before he set out to work; his writing is thus a very critical and judicious synthesis of the available sources. His texts on the history, geography, economy, geology, genealogy, and languages of Hungary are milestones in these disciplines. The culmination of his scientific career was the vast *Notitia Hungariae novae historico-geographica* (Historical and geographical knowledge about the new Hungary, 1735–42), of which only four volumes were ever published, describing the historical, political, administrative, ethnographical, and natural-scientific characteristics and features of some regions of the kingdom, including Bratislava, Zvolen, and Liptov. He is full of praise for the hard-working and gifted Slovak people, whose status as the first nation (for he sees the Magyars as the later settlers) he emphasizes, and he condemns those who attempt to diminish Slovak history. His national consciousness also found expression in his introduction to Pavel Doležal's *Grammatica Slavico-Bohemica* (Slovak-Czech grammar, 1746). As well, he inaugurated the first regularly published newspaper in the kingdom of Hungary: *Nova Posoniensia* (Bratislava news, 1721–22).

In the mid-eighteenth century, literary history made its début in the work of Michal Rotarides (1715–47), whose *Historiae Hungaricae literariae antiqui, medii atque recentioris aevi lineamenta* (A sketch of the literary history of Hungary during the old, middle, and newer ages, 1745) treats Slovak literature as one of the Hungarian literatures, and supplies biographical and bibliographical information on Slovak authors. This chronological account, beginning in the tenth century, ascribes the literary backwardness of Hungary to Turkish and Hapsburg oppression.

DEFENCE OF THE NATION AND ITS LANGUAGE AND PAN-SLAVISM

Following the few attempts (such as Bel's) to provide a justification for and defence of the Slovak nation and its language, a new genre of such apologetics sprang up, producing new and better arguments against those who tried to belittle the truth that the Slovaks had been settled on their territory long before the arrival of the Magyars and those who wanted to diminish the national aspirations of the Slovaks and of the other Slavs living in the kingdom of Hungary. Such writings may have strengthened the resolve of those who felt a certain inferiority *vis-à-vis* the ruling Magyar nation. Contemporary arguments stressed not so much the case of the Slovaks *per se*, but the cause of the Slavs, conjuring up the image of Slavdom (the entire family of Slavic nations) as a powerful force, an image that, in a hundred years, would become an important political fact in the eyes of Magyar politicians, despite the rather modest reality behind the concept.

One such work, *Murices ... sive Apologia* (Thorns ... or Defence), ascribed to Ján Baltazár Magin (1682–1735), is the answer to a polemical letter written by a professor at Trnava University, Michal Bencsik (1670–1728), in which he demeans the people of Trenčín, and Slovaks and Slavs in general. Bencsik's approach to the Slovak problem in Hungary was known as "the conquest" approach, as opposed to the "hospitality" approach. In the former, stress was put on the military conquest by the Magyars, which proved their strength and the consequent weakness of the Slovaks and other conquered Slavs in the kingdom. On the other hand, the latter considered the Slovaks (and Slavs in general) to be peaceful people who, after the initial defeat, proved to be good neighbours to the Magyars. In reality, the conquerors were forced to adopt the way of life (sedentary, as opposed to nomadic) and the religion (Christianity) of the conquered. Magin considers the ancient tradition of the saints Cyril and Methodius, and points out that in the kingdom of Hungary Slovaks have the same status as Hungarians (a point that he certainly would not have made a hundred years later) – indeed, they shared the same homeland. The Slovaks are described as members of the Slavic nation, but they have their own specific characteristics and a defined territory.

Lighter, more entertaining literature also appeared in the second half of the seventeenth century. Now that the Turkish nightmare and the religious persecution had ended, the time was ripe to take notice of the humorous prose that was circulating in Latin, which began to inspire imitators and original authors in Slovakia. Satirical and parodistic texts (political, religious, social), anecdotes, exempla, fables, and stories appeared in Latin (*Regulae insignis et incliti ordinis Bibiani* – Regulations of the glorious and famous order of drunkards) and Slovak (*Recept pre ženské pohlaví* – Recipe for the female sex).

Anecdotes were collected and published in anthologies such as *Democritus ridens* (Laughing Democritus, 1770), a work that inspired Jozef Ignác Bajza's (1755–1836) *Veselé účinky a rečení* (Merry sayings and stories, 1795), containing a variety of short stories, anecdotes, and exempla. The sources were equally varied, from classical literature (*Legenda aurea, Gesta Romanorum*) to Slovak folk-tales, and the stories concern a surprising cross-section of characters from a variety of classes, professions, and trades.

DRAMA

As in the Renaissance period, drama was limited to school plays; professional theatre and the private theatre of the nobility developed only toward the end of the Baroque period. Most of the school plays were written in Latin, and were based on biblical stories or dramatized moral principles, lives of martyrs or saints, and even pedagogical material.

Eliáš Ladiver (1633–86) was the most significant author of Protestant school plays written in Latin. Two significant works are ascribed to him: *Eleazar constans* (Faithful Eleazar, 1668) and *Papinianus tetragonos* (Courageous Papinianus, 1669). The first concerns a man with unshakable faith, a topic dear to the persecuted Protestants of the time. The other is the story of the Roman lawyer Papinianus, who was executed by Marcus Aurelius Severus Caracalla after he refused to provide the emperor with a justification for the murder of the emperor's brother.

Slovak secular drama is represented by *Tragoedia neb Hra smutná, prežalostná* (Tragedy, or a sad, sorrowful play, 1728), an interesting allegory in which Truth and Courage battle with Satan (lies and injustice). Apart from the religious content, there are some sharp observations of the social life of the time, particularly the widening gap between the professed religious morality and the reality of wordly injustice.

Slovak Catholic (Jesuit) plays were more inclined to secularism, but often this was merely functional, as in the didactic school plays, designed to enhance teaching. A rather striking exception to this practice was a Latin-Slovak Jesuit play entitled *Catharina Gurzianorum regina, proprio sanguine purpurata, theatro data – Caterina, královna gurziánska, vlastní krve ozdobená, na divadlo predstavená* (Catherine, queen of Georgia, decorated by her own blood, presented on the stage, 1701), a celebration of martyrdom based on a Christian legend with a wide range of sources and allusions. Most of them are rather exotic (the Georgian queen is helped by Minerva, Iris, and Vulcan), and this mixture of Greek mythology and Oriental adventure story may have been an adaptation of a German play.

Foreign theatre companies started to tour in Slovakia; Austrian and Italian companies first appeared in the seventeenth century, followed by Bohemian troupes, and they performed in Bratislava and Košice. Toward the end of the eighteenth century, interest in the theatre among the nobility and the townfolk was on the rise. The first (wooden) theatre in Bratislava was built in 1741, and a permanent building was added in 1776. Private theatres built by noblemen opened in Bratislava, and in the country seats of the nobility, in Dolná Krupa and Hlohovec. The touring companies performed Moliére, Klopstock, Lessing, Goethe, and Shakespeare in German. The operatic repertoire featured Pergolesi and Mozart.

Folk drama, having grown from the Passion-plays and Christmas pageants, was enriched with the addition of *Hra o sv. Dorote* (A play about St Dorothea). The martyrdom of St Dorothea is presented with a cast of characters including the King, the Angel, the Executioner, and the Devil, and the central conflict is between the King and Dorothea, who would not give up her faith. The original story has been "carnivalized" – to use Bakhtin's term – to a certain extent, so that it became a folk play in which justice is locked in combat with wordly power.

4 Classicism (1780–1828)

If there are periods in Slovak history when it seems that nothing happens for centuries, it is also true that there are decades when the work of ages is accomplished. In less than a hundred years after 1780, in place of a few dreamers who desperately tried to prove to their own people that they in fact existed as a nation, who tried to revive the languge and literature of a nation dispirited by a millennium of oppression, there was a well-established Slovak literature. The Slovak language proved flexible enough to communicate not only poetry and prose, but all scientific disciplines. More importantly, there was among the leaders of Slovakia a well-established consensus about the nation that no longer had to be proved to anyone. Perhaps because of this, oppression of the Slovaks intensified, as action led inexorably to reaction. Despite any impression to the contrary, the Hungarian authorities were well aware of the existence of this new consensus, for they redoubled their efforts to smother it. But it was by now too advanced to eradicate.

Classicism, as an international cultural phenomenon also known as neo-Classicism or pseudo-Classicism, is connected to the philosophy of rationalism and the general atmosphere of the Enlightenment, with its excesses of anti-religious, anti-monarchist, and revolutionary radicalism culminating in the charnel-houses of the French Revolution. Aesthetically, it is a retreat from the triumphalism of the Baroque style, with its luxurious ornamentation and cloud-like formlessness. The austerity of Graeco-Roman simplicity evoked during the Renaissance made a come-back. This was also the era influenced by Napoleon, although the Napoleonic complex expressed in literature as a justification for various types of nationalism and rebelliousness, as well as the glorification of the underdog – or the "little man," or the parvenu – came later, with Romanticism.

The general trend toward atomization of medieval unity was further developed in this age, as demonstrated by the ascendance of secular literature over religious literature. The new pan-Europeanism proclaimed by Napoleon had, in fact, led to rebellions in subjected nations (Poland, Hungary) and to further division. But such events were hardly foreseeable in the heady, if not euphoric, beginning of this period, which was dominated by an unexpected and dramatic liberalism from above in the historic decrees issued by Joseph II, the Holy Roman Emperor.

The 1781 Decree of Tolerance went a long way toward dissipating the consequences of the Reformation by making the Protestant church equal with the Catholic church (though complete equality came only in 1790, during the rule of Leopold II). A few weeks later, Joseph II abolished serfdom, and in 1782 he struck a blow against the Catholic church by closing some seven hundred monasteries, limiting church holidays, and organizing priestly training in so-called general seminaries. This weakening of the powers of the nobility and the church resulted in a rather ominous concentration of power in the state. It was at this point that the formidable administrative structure of the Austrian bureaucracy, which found its definitive literary apotheosis in the works of Kafka and Musil, was born. Joseph II, however, was quite likely motivated by good intentions. For example, he made his patrimony more efficient, more competitive, and less backward relative to other countries, particularly Prussia. But his most fateful decision was to use the German language in his administration. This had disastrous consequences for Slovak culture and galvanized Slovak nationalists.

The kingdom of Hungary was the only country in which Latin was used for administrative purposes. When Joseph II made German the primary language of the empire, he set in motion a process that led to the substitution of Hungarian for Latin, although this took some fifty years. The very announcement, however, made it clear that national languages would be paramount. The age of nations had arrived in Central Europe. The kingdom of Hungary included many nationalities, but it was in the interest of the Hungarians (Magyars) to disregard them (especially the Slovaks). Although they themselves had had to fight for their rights against the Austrians, they were blind to identical arguments by the Slovaks. Once the ambiguous energies of nationalism were released in the French Revolution, however, Hungarians and Slovaks in Austria listened and acted.

Suddenly, it was vital to gather all the arguments that the apologists for the Slovak nation, Slavdom, and the Slovak language had produced. Each historical event concerning Slovaks and Slavs suddenly gained new importance. It became an urgent task to codify the language, since it was now the most important attribute of nationhood. Another urgent task was to spread the news. Heretofore, literary, historical, and linguistic issues were the concern of a few savants and enthusiasts; in the age of mass mobilization introduced by the French Revolution, this was not good enough. And so this unexpected, sudden, and vigorous movement on the historical stage had a direct mobilizing influence on Slovak literature. It is not an exaggeration to say that but for the work of the men of literature, the existence of the Slovak nation and state would be an impossibility. Thus, in this period, Slovak literature began to assume the task, admittedly an extraliterary one, of nation-building. The men to whom this difficult task fell were Jozef Ignác Bajza, Anton Bernolák, Juraj Fándly, Juraj Palkovič, and the other builders of the national revival.

This new linguistic reality led to a revived interest in the Great Moravian Empire. That Great Moravia had been the most powerful state east of the Frankish Empire, that the first Slavic literature had appeared there, and that the disciples of saints Cyril and Methodius had brought Christianity and education to other Slavs led not only to a sense of pride, but also to the realization that Slovaks were a part of the greater Slav family. It is not surprising, then, that in this period there were Slovaks who defined themselves as Slavs, although they still considered themselves Slovaks and, more importantly, believed that the Slovaks were the heirs to Great Moravia. Although it may seem strange that the Slovaks considered that ancient period of such importance, to the Slovaks themselves it was clear: remove the hiatus of Hungarian rule and you arrive at history. Consequently, Slovaks, who up to then were Hungarian patriots, suddenly saw the possibility of identifying themselves as Slovak patriots. They had good models in the Poles and Croats.

Juraj Papánek (b. 1738) was a Slovak historian who lived among Croats and was impressed by the unambiguous national consciousness of the Croat nobility. When he wrote his major work, *Historia gentis Slavae. De Regno regibusque Slavorum atque cumprisci civilis et ecclesiastici, tum huis aevi statu gentis Slavae* (The history of the Slovak nation. About the kingdom and the kings of Slovaks, 1780), he was writing as much for the Croats as for the Slovaks. Reading about this once-mighty state with Slavic rulers and realizing that it had been centred in Slovakia had a powerful influence on learned Slovaks. Papánek decisively discredited reigning Magyar theories about the conquest of the Slovaks, basing his work on unimpeachable historical sources, pointing out the extent of the Great Moravian Empire, as well as the fact that it was defeated only by an assault in which the Magyar forces were helpted by the Franks an the Czechs. It was not shameful to be defeated under such circumstances. Papánek also made a great impression with his portrait of Svätopluk as a strong leader.

Another interpretation of Slovak history was provided by Juraj Sklenár (1745–90), author of *Vetustissimus Magnae Moraviae situs et primus in eam Hungarorum ingressus et incursus* (The oldest situation of Great Moravia and the first arrival of the Magyars, 1784). Sklenár held the unusual opinions that the centre of Great Moravia was in Bulgaria, from which it expanded to include (by treaty) Slovakia, and that the Magyars never actually conquered the territory between the Danube and the Tatra Mountains. His debate with a professor of history from Buda was acrimonious, and the consensus was and is that Sklenár was wrong. However, he did defend the idea of natiónal equality, writing, "He who creates hate of other nations is seeking the destruction of this state and everything that goes with it and aims at the destruction of the foundations on which Hungary stands. Such a man is dangerous to the fatherland."

These historical writings were a prelude to the appearance of a number of powerful writers who were unhappy with the fact that the Slovaks did not have a single literary language, but that a number of dialects were used for oral communication, while writing was done in Slovakized Czech. The time had come to deal with this problem, and several attempts were made to produce a Slovak grammar. The pioneer in this venture was Jozef Ignác Bajza, who was followed by Anton Bernolák and his circle.

PRELUDE TO THE LITERATURE OF CLASSICISM

Jozef Ignác Bajza (1755–1836)

Bajza was the author of the first Slovak novel, *René mláďenca príhodi a skúsenosti* (The adventures and experiences of a young man called René, 1783, 1785. When the second volume was published, church authorities bought out the entire edition; only a few copies of the novel survived. Inspired by Fenelon's *Telemachus* (1699), Bajza's work is a mixture of travelogue and picaresque novel. The plot is a rather chaotic one: in the first volume, René looks for his long-lost sister by setting out from Venice for Tripoli, where he finds her, but he loses her again and must cross another sea to find her. His ship is wrecked; he is saved, but at the price of becoming a slave. He experiences an erotic interlude with the beautiful Hadixa, for which he is sentenced to death. He escapes and manages to return to Venice, where he finally finds his sister and his parents. In the second volume, the action shifts to Europe, which René tours with a companion. He travels from Italy to Slovakia, where he casts a critical eye on the prevailing conditions. When René then visits Slovak village, with its drunkenness, poverty, and superstition, Bajza stays true to his initial intention: to provide not only adventures, but also a true picture of the world. René (and the reader) next finds out about the family life of a Lutheran bishop, about a Jewish tavern-keeper, and about a stingy Catholic priest. Some of these portraits are vividly drawn and must have pushed the authorities to act against Bajza's novel.

In 1794, Bajza published the controversial *Slovenské dvojnásobné epigrammata* (Slovak epigrams), ironically referring to Anton Bernolák's new Slovak Learned Society, of which he was not a member, but from which, as a proud man who was not approached, he felt excluded. His attempt to arrive at the first literary Slovak was the target of a withering attack by Bernolák and Juraj Fándly, two leading personalities of the early revival. They accused Bajza of introducing a Slovak that was a hodge-podge of "Czech-Moravian-Polish-Croatian-Ukrainian," and criticized his orthography. Their rancour may have arisen from their perception that Bajza had not behaved in a gentlemanly manner toward them: when they were in trouble with the authorities, Bajza, a priest like they were, did not take their side.

Nevertheless, Bajza was the first to see the need to ameliorate the language situation in Slovakia; even if he failed, it was a worthy attempt. His novel can be judged highly; that it was prevented from playing its proper role in the history of the Slovak novel was hardly his fault.

Anton Bernolák (1762–1813)

Like Bajza, Bernolák's great attempt to establish literary Slovak failed, but not before some of the outstanding men of letters of Bernolák's time, including Juraj Fándly and Ján Hollý, accepted it and used it for literary purposes. Bernolák's Slovak was based on the West Slovak dialect, which was spoken by the people who lived in the administrative centre of Slovakia – in and around Bratislava and Trnava. Because it is closer to Czech than the Central Slovak dialect that was eventually codified as literary Slovak, it could be termed a transitional step, a sort of unconscious compromise.

In 1787, Bernolák published *Dissertatio philologico-critica de litteris Slavorum* (A critical linguistic disseration regarding Slovak letters), adding to it his proposed *Orthographia*, and stated that his work was addressed to the many readers who wanted to see their language cleansed of the pronunciation and grammatical errors introduced into Slovak from the Czech language. This statement ended the ambivalence that many must have felt regarding the Czech language. At the same time, it was the first step in what would become a rather bitter misunderstanding among Czech friends of Slovakia and among some key Slovak personalities, who feared that by detaching themselves from the well-functioning body of Czech culture, whose language (in the form of Slovakized Czech) they were using for literary purposes, they risked sudden cultural isolation.

Bernolák introduced a phonetic orthography (as opposed to an etymological one) and, in 1790, he supported his argument with a voluminous work, *Grammatica slavica* (Slovak grammar). Curiously, he saw correctly that the best foundation for the Slovak language would be the Central Slovak dialect, but he declined to move in that direction because of problems he anticipated with his Trnava publisher, who was used to the West Slovak dialect. Conscious of the importance of etymology, he wrote *Etymologia vocum slavicarum* (Slovak etymology, 1791), then crowned his life's work with the posthumously published *Slowar Slovenskí-Česko-Latinsko-Nemecko-Uherskí* (Slovak-Czech-Latin-German-Hungarian dictionary, 1825–27), an enormous six-volume work.

Bernolák's burst of creative energy underscores the strange characteristic of Slovak history, with its long stretches of relative inactivity, followed by a short period in which the work of generations was somehow accomplished. In Bernolák's time, however, the conditions were propitious: to the explosion of interest in Slovak history was added an even more significant attempt to rectify the lack of a literary language. Although Bernolák's Slovak did not last, it was in fact the literary language until the arrival of "Štúr's Slovak," in 1843.

It all started in the Bratislava general seminary. When Bernolák arrived there after his theological studies in nearby Vienna, he found a group of like-minded Slovaks: the seminarians were grouped by nationalities here, and so the Slovaks got to know each other and formed a fraternity, which eventually grew into the Slovak Learned Society, founded in Trnava in 1792. Within three years, the society had 450 members all over Slovakia. Since most of them were priests, they had real potential to raise the national consciousness of their parishioners. Disappointingly, however, the society went into a decline, although some activists continued enthusiastically. A key role in the society was played by Juraj Fándly.

Juraj Fándly (1750–1811)

It is often said that Bernolák owed a great deal to the tireless activity and practical disposition of his elder, Juraj Fándly. In Fándly, the practical abilities of a promoter of Bernolák's Slovak who understood how to approach the simple people was combined with a poet's talent. He stood with his people in their times of trouble for a very simple reason – he himself came from a very poor family.

Fándly was born in Častá, near Trnava. After his theological studies in Buda, he became a chaplain in Sereď, and then, in 1780, a priest in Naháč. After twenty-seven years, he had to retire because of poor eyesight and a nervous condition. He returned to Častá, where he died poor and alone, abandoned and forgotten by his friends.

The greatest moment of Fándly's life was his meeting with the young priests of the Bratislava general seminary, led by Bernolák. By that time, Fándly already had his own ideas, but he willingly joined Bernolák's society and embraced his concept of the Slovak language. He produced the first substantial literary work written in Bernolák's Slovak, a rather controversial work entitled *Dúvěrná zmluva medzi mníchom a diablom o prvních počátkoch, o starodávních, aj o včulajších premenách reholníckych, kterú spísal ve čtyrech stránkach pre mladých prešporských kňazov Juro Fándly* (A confidential contract between a monk and a devil about the origin, the ancient times, and the present changes in religious communities, written in four parts by Juro Fándly for the young priests of Pressburg, 1789). It expressed Fándly's strong support of Joseph II's reforms, including the closure of the monasteries of the mendicant orders.

Fándly realized the significance of this work and stated that he wrote "so that once and for all in this learned, enlightened eighteenth century of ours, one of the most ancient languages can be brought to light from the darkness with proper grammar, usage, and orthography." The book was published by Bernolák's society. Fándly ran into trouble when Bajza notified the church authorities about it, going so far as to volunteer to condemn it as harmful to religion. The church authorities solicited another opinion, which was equally negative, so Fándly was requested to abandon literature.

However, this did not stop Fándly from his work with the people, whom he saw as exploited, condemned to poverty, and poorly educated. In 1792, he published a "Farmer's Almanac" (*Pilní domajší a polní hospodár*), in which he gave the populace useful advice on how to improve its lot by starting small manufactures, instituting proper planning, and combining its forces. He believed that economic progress would further cultural development.

In his practical handbooks, Fándly managed to include some information about Slovak history and the tradition of saints Cyril and Methodius. He tried to make his readers conscious of belonging to a nation that should partake of the opportunities that followed Joseph II's reforms.

Another of Fándly's commitments was to awaken feelings of national pride in Slovaks who did have a good education and who were – due to the uncertainty of the political situation – at a crossroads, forced with a choice of literary language between Czech, German, or Hungarian. For these readers, Fándly wrote *Compendiata Historia Gentis Slavae* (Concise history of the Slovak nation, 1793), focusing on both Slovak history and Slovak literature.

Fándly's call to action comes from his introduction to the second volume of the almanac:

> Brothers! Think about that muddy and gloomy century that Slovaks who lived before us had to face: now we're facing an enlightened time. Let us try to raise our nation, our good name, our descendants with our language, our writings, our books – if not to the golden age, then at least to the silver age! Let us make an effort, let us encourage each other, let us add the will, combine our strength and power.

This is also a fitting summary of the age of Bernolák, Bajza, Fándly, and Juraj Palkovič. It truly was the silver age of Slovak literature, pointing to the golden age that was to arrive within a few decades.

The Movement for Czecho-Slovak Literature

While Bajza, Bernolák, and Fándly, their followers, and the Slovak Learned Society were keenly aware of the need for resolving the language problem, their desire for some sort of national cohesion and integration was not shared by the Lutheran Slovaks. As I have noted, they were using the old-Czech Kralice Bible for their services, and for them it did not seem unnatural to use Czech, albeit a Slovakized, fossilized, and archaic Czech, while in Bohemia living Czech was developing and undergoing reforms. This does not mean that they did not "feel" like Slovaks. They even insisted on calling the language they used "Czecho-Slovak," and the literature created in it "Czecho-Slovak literature." They were historically oriented toward Czech literature, which they, with good reason, considered their own. After all, had not the best Lutheran Slovak authors enriched Czech literature with their work?

Thus their good relationship with some outstanding Czechs (Dobrovský, Puchmajer) encouraged them not to feel isolated. This special situation illuminates the dilemma of such Slovak literary giants as Pavol Jozef Šafárik and Ján Kollár. The activities of Bernolák's society must have inspired the Slovak Lutherans to act.

In 1793, a year after the establishment of the Slovak Learned Society, Jur Ribay proposed the Societas slavobohemica (Czechoslovak Society), but it took ten years for his plan to come to fruition. This was the age of such societies; in the following decade, a number of them sprang up in various regions. More importantly, in 1801, the Lutheran superintendent, Martin Hamaliar (1750–1812), founded the Institute of Czechoslovak Language and Literature in Bratislava, with the purpose of providing a chair of Czech at the Lutheran lyceum in Bratislava, with Juraj Palkovič as the professor of "Czechoslovak language and literature."

A somewhat special place in the period, quite aside from linguistic and nationalistic concerns, belongs to Samuel Tešedík (1742–1820), a brilliant teacher and a disciple of A.H. Francke and J.H. Pestalozzi. Tešedík played an important role in educational work, providing practical instruction on rational methods of agriculture. He also organized reading clubs, perhaps the most important link in the chain that led to the period of the national revival. It was the patient work of countless pioneers such as Fándly and Tešedík that prepared the soil for this next and most important age of Slovak literature.

Augustin Doležal (1737–1802)

Doležal, a nephew of Pavol Doležal, the author of the Czech grammar, was a Protestant pastor who studies theology in Altsdorf, where the philosopher G.W. Leibnitz had studied. He was an enthusiastic supporter of the Josephian reforms and wrote an encomium on the emperor, expressing his happiness over the Decree on Tolerance.

Doležal's major work, a philosophical-theological poem in thirty cantos of 259 stanzas each, *Pamětná celému světu tragoedie* (A tragedy the whole world remembers, 1791), is a massive composition dealing with the problem of science and religion. In the tradition of such philosophical poems as Milton's *Paradise Lost* and Klopstock's *Messiah*, Doležal tackles the problem of Original Sin in the form of a dialogue between Adam, Eve, and Seth. His rationalistic justification uses the following argument:

> Mind! Know God's world.
> The world, everyone should know, is nothing but
> the chain and linkage of final causes …

. . . .
Each cause is the root of potentialities
and never can stay wholly idle;
it has to act! And where there is action,
there's life, there's power, not death!

Doležal explains the world on the basis of the Bible, and, true to the rationalism of the Enlightenment, builds *Pamětná ... tragoedie* on the philosophy of deism. If the punishment of mankind is death and work, then it is "action," to use Doležal's word, that justifies the divine dispensation, for action leads to life, which conquers even death itself. There are similarities with the conclusion drawn in Madách's *Human Tragedy* and Goethe's *Faust*.

Juraj Palkovič (1769–1850)

One of the first secular poets, whose arrival on the literary scene was marked by his collection of poetry entitled *Múza ze Slovenských hor* (Muse from the Slovak mountains, 1801), Palkovič raised great expectations. He had also, and very credibly, begun the work of translating Homer. Although he advertised that other collections of poetry would follow, *Múza* was his last poetic effort. Nor did he continue with his translation of Homer. Nevertheless, he did start something that was to grow into a considerable poetic heritage during Štúr's time – the cult of home, nestled in the Slovak mountains, cradled in the valleys.

Appointed as a professor of Czech at the Lutheran lyceum, Palkovič switched his attention to philological concerns and published *Česko-nemecko-latinský slovník* (Czech-German-Latin dictionary, 1820, 1821), which was based on *Kraličtina*, the Czech of the Kralice Bible.

Palkovič's lectures in Latin on Czech literature were quite unpopular and somewhat irregular. If one is to believe Ján Kollár, he did not hear him lecture during the five years of his stay in Bratislava. Palkovič was a better publisher, and a patriot, as his good relations with the Slovak Learned Society testify. He published some very popular calendars and much educational literature.

Palkovič also tried his hand at comedy, with *Dva buchy a tri šuchy. Slovenská komédia k zasmání se pro pána i pro sedláka* (Two blows and three pushes: A Slovak comedy for the amusement of gentlemen as well as peasants, 1800). It is interesting that despite his "Czecho-Slovak" position, Palkovič wrote this work in a very strongly Slovakized Czech.

Palkovič also assisted Štúr, claiming some secret meetings of Štúr's circle as his own and defending Štúr against his enemies. He was a very successful organizer, leaving a solid oeuvre, and he did much for the good of Slovak literature, as well as the Slovak cause, however he may have conceived it. A statement of his summarizes his contribution fairly: "I was never ashamed and never will be ashamed to be called publicly a Slovak, a friend of the Slavic nation, a Slavic writer – though some boors are. I also have the inner satisfaction to have published, by myself, twenty-five various Slovak books, having overcome many obstacles and much evil."

Bohuslav Tablic (1769–1832)

A graduate of the Lutheran lyceum in Bratislava and the University of Jena, where he learned English, Tablic spent most of his life as a pastor in Kostolné Moravce. Unlike other typically penniless pastors and priests whose interest in literature only increased their impoverishment, Tablic was relatively wealthy, and this enabled him to do much for Slovak literature. Like Palkovič, he saw its future in a close relationship with Czech literature, and he was also a partisan of the concept of "Czecho-Slovak" language and literature, although by this time events had made the concept somewhat outmoded.

Tablic aspired to a professorship of philology, and would doubtless have made a better candidate than Palkovič, simply on account of his erudition and his scholarly temperament, if not his ability to financially aid publishing ventures. But it was not to be. Nevertheless, he made his mark as a poet, translator, publisher, editor, literary historiographer, and literary theoretician.

His collection of poetry, *Poezye Bohuslava Tablice* (The poetry of Bohuslav Tablic, 1806–12), promotes the ideal of the *via media*, the quiet, comfortable life expressed in the motto "Old wine, old books, old friends."

> My and my friends' main concen would be
> to promote the success of the Slovak language,
> we would publish great works,
> make a pleasant home for the Muses,
> they would sing Slovak songs in Hungary ...
> – if I could see Slavia flourish so beautifully,
> rising to the heavens shining with glory ...
> Atropos could cut short
> the time of my life thread.

The collection also contains horrific ballads, an unexpected turn from the sober-minded and rational scholar, who was influenced by the popular English Gothic.

Tablic translated German poetry, as well as Shakespeare's *Hamlet* monologue and works by Oliver Goldsmith, Alexander Pope, and other English writers. He was the first Slovak translator of modern poetry, collected in *Anglické múzy v česko-slovenském oděvu* (English muses in Czecho-Slovak dress, 1831). Also of significance is his translation of Nicholas Boileau's *Umění básnírské* (The art of poetry, 1832).

As a literary historiographer, Tablic penned *Paměti československých básnířův* (The memoir of Czecho-Slovak poets) which he included in each volume of his poetry. This was the first attempt at a systematic treatment of older Slovak literature, beginning in the sixteenth century. He also published an anthology of older Slovak poetry, *Slovenští veršovci* (Slovak poets, 1805, 1809).

Tablic enriched Slovak literature bringing to it his exposure to the wider European context, but he remained deeply committed to the promotion of Slovak literature, old and new. While his literary efforts were not particularly impressive, the sum total of his activities as a translator, historiographer of literature, publisher, and philanthropist (he left some money to the slovak Lutheran schools, where, as in Bratislava, the revivalist movement was being born) gave him a distinguished place in the history of Slovak literature.

THE LITERATURE OF CLASSICISM

Napoleon's army sowed death, but also ideas of equality, which made a greater impression on people than the notions of liberty and fraternity. Most importantly, he awakened in young people the hope that by their own actions they could change the status quo. Suddenly, nothing seemed impossible. The iconography of classicism is confirmed by the huge canvasses of David. The gigantomania of the architecture of the time (the unrealized French Temple of Unity, for instance) was the civilian equivalent of the magalomania of the march on Russia. This was a time of great deeds and great projects, and such a time demanded great, instantly "classic" works of literature as well.

All Slavs were becoming restless, sensing that their hour was coming. Even Western prophets, like the German writer Johann Gottfried Herder, were telling them that the fickle goddess of history was about to smile upon them. And then Russia defeated Napoleon and the Russian army was in Paris. Suddenly, King Jan Sobieski of Poland, the defender of Vienna who had defeated the Turks, a Slav, was remembered, together with Peter the Great, who defeated the Swedes at Poltava, and now Russia was not only victorious, but a member of the European "Holy Alliance," with Prussia and Austria! These were revolutionary, heady times. And it did not matter yet to the Slovak patriots that the purpose of the alliance was to keep the spirit of rebellion down. The main thing was that Russia, a Slavic nation, was now accepted – it was a member of the club, so to speak.

To be a Slav was suddenly respectable, but it also demanded great deeds. The burgeoning nationalism came in two varieties: defensive, aimed at preserving language and culture (Poland), and aggressive, disregarding similar claims by subjected nations (Hungary). For example, when Ján Kollár published his idea of Slavic reciprocity, he was attacked by a Hungarian poet, Mihály Vőrősmarty, who stated that this was a reactionary idea because it helped to spread Russian influence. On the other hand, one has to understand the Hungarians' position – their claustrophobic feeling of being surrounded, stranded in the Slavic sea! They must have considered any "pan-Slav" ideas to be of the utmost danger to Hungary, for Slavs outnumbered Hungarians. However, this claustrophobia did not exist until the 1830s, for until then, they too considered themselves underdogs *vis-à-vis* Austria and thought of the Slovaks as potential allies in that conflict.

The search for a new homeland, a new *patria*, was on. Some found it by moving even closer to the Czechs (Šafárik, Kollár), others by continuing the direction charted by Bernolák and the Slovak Learned Society (Hollý and others). In this great, even tragic division the arguments for the first of the second option weighed less than did poetry. Today, looking at this split and knowing how it was resolved, it seems that there was only one logical way, the way of the Slovak language, with Slovakia as the homeland – not a new homeland, but one that had been there from time immemorial.

Pavel Jozef Šafárik (1795–1861)

The comet-like arrival of the nineteen-year-old Šafárik on the Slovak literary scene with his *Tatranská múza s lýrou slovanskou* (The muse of the Tatra with a slavic lyre, 1814) was hailed by Palkovič and also by the great Czech revivalist Jungmann, who was impressed by Šafárik's knowledge of the Czech language. They did not know that some of these poems were written when Šafárik was sixteen. A precocious boy, he was encouraged by his father, a Lutheran pastor, to excel as a Latinist; when he was in the Kežmarok lyceum he concentrated on classical and German literature. At the same time, he was trying his hand at Czech poetry. He published his first collection before leaving for Jena, at the time a Mecca of Slovak Lutheran university study, mostly in theology.

From Jena, Šafárik continued to contribute poetry to a Viennese Czech publication. He neglected theology and studied linguistics, philosophy, and history; captivated by Greek drama, he translated Aristophanes' *Clouds,* as well as Schiller's tragedy *Mary Stuart* (1831). At this time, however, he was deeply influenced by nationalist ideas and started to drift away from writing poetry.

In 1817, Šafárik published *Proclamation to the Slavs,* in which he wrote of the Slavdom that he saw in the process of awakening. He reminded his readers of Herder's *Stimmen der Volker in Liedern* (1778, 1779), the formative work that inspired Slavs to turn their attention to their folk literature, which, until then, they had neglected in the effort to become well versed in classical literature. As personal models, Šafárik mentioned Goethe; Ivan Prac, the collector of Russian songs; and Vuk Štefanovič Karadzič, the publisher of Serbian songs. These treasures had always been available, but had somehow been neglected. In an atmosphere of growing nationalism, each nation was trying to take stock of the treasury of its literature, and Herder re-evaluated the contribution of folk poetry, making it seem even more valuable than learned poetry. In this connection, Krčméry speaks of the tradition of Rousseau, Mistral, and Gessner and their call, "Back to Nature!"

Šafárik called on his readers to collect folk literature, reasoning that its language was a pure and living one and should be recorded as such. To set an example, he published thirteen folk songs. His appeal had a tremendous effect, encouraging the gathering of the still uncollected Slovak folk literature, which was published as it was recorded, and not translated into Czech. This in itself had an impact on the Czech-Slovak language controversy, although Šafárik did not at the time (and perhaps not even later) consider the obvious: if an entire people *speaks* like that, why *write* differently?

After his studies in Jena, Šafárik returned to Bratislava, where he became a tutor. There, he met František Palacký, also a tutor and one of the key personalities in the Czech national revival. Together, they wrote an influential work "in six letters": *Počátkove českého básnictví obzvláště prosodie* (The beginnings of Czech poetry, especially prosody, 1818). Both Palacký and Šafárik were unhappy with the state of Czech poetry and proposed a radical change, suggesting that Czech poetry use syllabo-tonic verse instead of the "accentuated" verse that was then employed. Ironically, even as they were writing, Ján Hollý was already writing in syllabo-tonic verse, producing the historic epic whose absence they bewailed in their pamphlet.

In 1819, Šafárik was appointed the principal of and professor at a Serbian *gymnasium* (secondary school) in Novi Sad, and for the next forty years he lived outside Slovakia, first in Serbia, then, from 1833 on, in Prague. There is no doubt that the long time away from his country while he endured poverty, family problems, and personal sickness further alienated him from Slovakia, but never from his Slavic patriotism, as his steady stream of publications shows. First, he published a collection of Slovak folk-songs, *Písně světské lidu slovenského v Uhřích* (Folk-songs of Slovak people in Hungary, 1823), a venture that Ján Kollár continued.

Šafárik's next work, published in German, was the first comparative history of Slavic languages and literatures. *Geschichte der Slawischen Sprache und Literatur nach allen Mundarten* (The History of Slavic language and literature, 1826), established, for a wide international audience, the claims of Slavic culture, praised its level of accomplishment, and predicted a great future for it. More important, this work became a cornerstone of Slavic linguistics, literature, and general culture. Šafárik recognized the specificity of the Slovak language and even had a word of praise for Bernolák's movement, although he expressed the wish that they would return to the Czech language.

Šafárik's *Slovanské starožitnosti* (Slavic antiquities, 1837) was published with the financial help of the Russian historian Mikhail P. Pogodin. This far-reaching reconstruction, in more than a thousand pages, of the history of the Slavs from their beginnings to the end of the tenth century produced an even greater impression. In a companion work, *Slovanský národopis* (Slavic ethnography 1842), Šafárik retreated from the statement that he had made in the 1820s about the specificity of the Slovak language, calling it an "Ugro-Slovak" dialect of Czech. In his overview of literatures, he mentioned the Slovak literature of the Slovak Learned Society, and even gave it a sympathetic evaluation, but spoke of "Czechoslovak literature," still hoping for some compromise solution that would preserve the linguistic unity of the two languages.

His *On the Origin and the Domicile of the Glagolitic Script* (1858), published in German, was a definitive study of Old Slavic manuscripts proving the primacy of Glagolitic script at a time when the Cyrillic was thought to have preceded it. His last, posthumously published work was his German-language *History of the South Slavic Literatures* (1856).

Šafárik's last years were tragic. Those for whom he toiled for so many years did not seem to appreciate his work when he needed help, understanding, and appreciation. In his prime, a constant flow of visitors came from abroad to see him; the Russian tsar sent a delegation to see him; he was invited to visit many countries. He always refused, so deeply committed was he to his mission. But he ended his life neglected, poor, disappointed, and dispirited: in May 1860, he tried to commit suicide by jumping into the river Moldau. He died a year later.

Ján Kollár (1793–1852)

When, in 1818, Šafárik and Palacký complained that there was no great poet in their literature, they could not have known that in few years, the first sonnets of the greatest epic of Czech and Slovak literature would be published. With Kollár's *Slávy dcera* (The daughter of Slava, 1824), a new era began in Slovak literature. Along with Ján Hollý, Kollár exemplifies the best of Slovak classical poetry.

It was the classics – Horace, Virgil, Cicero, Quintilian – that Kollár first fell in love with when he discovered his passion for poetry: "This passion was so fierce that I would read a classic even in church, during the singing or a sermon, hiding it carefully in my hat." His youth was far from carefree. His father, a man of some education, a mayor and notary, wanted him to stay in his home town, Mošovce, but Kollár ran away and put himself through school by working as a tutor. He arrived in Bratislava in 1812; when he secured the position of supervisor of an orphanage, his situation improved and he took lessons in French, Italian, and English and added to his knowledge of Latin and German. While in Bratislava he heard of Napoleon's defeat in Russia. This made him a life-long convert to Slavdom.

From Bratislava, Kollár moved to Banská Bystrica, in the heart of Slovakia, where he met Samuel Rožnay, who helped to acquaint him with Slavic literature. Thus equipped, Kollár left for two years' study in Jena. The stay in Jena after the Napoleonic wars was a heady experience: Kollár witnessed German students publicly advocating the unification of Germany. As the first in a long line of Slovak Lutheran students of theology in Germany, the inquisitive and very observant Kollár could not help but notice that in the area around Jena and elsewhere in Saxony, there were place names of clearly Slavic origin, but no Slavs. This made a deep impression on him. He suddenly felt the weight of history: here was palpable evidence of the German movement eastward. He thought about the German cities in Slovakia, which were only slowly letting in Slovaks, and wondered if perhaps a similar fate was not in store for his own nation. Helping a sick priest in the nearby village of Lobeda, Kollár fell in love with the cleric's daughter, Friederike Wilhelmina Schmidt. After the death of the priest, Kollár was offered the parish, but he refused it because he wanted to work for his own nation. Young Friederike was fearful of moving to Hungary. And so, with a broken heart, Kollár left the place of his greatest inspiration, which led to his greatest epic. He would have to wait until 1835 to marry his beloved Friederike.

Kollár was then sent to Budapest, to serve as chaplain to the populous Slovak Lutheran community. This entailed some unpleasant skirmishing with the resident German Lutheran community, and there was little time for poetry, but what he had written under the powerful inspiration of Jena was published by Jungmann in Prague in 1821, as *Básně Jána Kollára* (Poems of Ján Kollár). The collection of eighty-six poems was an instant success, as much for its fresh and frank expression of the emotions of love as for its courageous call for the mobilization and unity of Slavs. The book was censored by Jungmann, for several of the poems were considered seditious.

This collection served as the basis for *Slávy dcera*, in which 150 poems were divided into three cantos named after three rivers: the Sala, the Elbe, and the Danube. The whole composition was prefaced by a prologue, the beauty of which was one of the main reasons for the epic's success. In the prologue, Kollár alchemized his love for Friederike Schmidt into something absolute and ideal – the daughter of the goddess Slava, called Mina. The underpinning of this great glorification of Slavdom, freedom, and love is the philosophy of history that Kollár borrowed from Herder. The lyrical hero, the unhappy lover of Mina, is also the tribune who spreads the message of the great future of the Slavic idea.

Encouraged by the tremendous success of this work Kollár published an expanded version, comprising six hundred poems divided into seven cantos: Sala, Elbe, Rhine, Moldau, Danube, Lethe, and Acheron. This work, which borrowed compositionally from Dante's *Divine Comedy*, was not as resounding a success as the first edition.

Equally important for the history of Slovak literature was Kollár's role as a collector and publisher of Slovak folk-songs (a project initiated by Šafárik). *Národnie zpievanky* (Folk-songs, 1834, 1835) became a textbook for the romantic period and one of the sources for literary Slovak. Kollár's proposal, entitled *O literárni vzájemnosti mezi kmeny a nářečími slávskymi* (Regarding literary reciprocity among the Slavic tribes and dialects, 1836), suggests that all educated Slavs should learn four main Slavic languages, and regularly exchange all of their cultural accomplishments.

The last period of Kollár's life found him divorced from Slovakian affairs, and from literature. Instead, he roamed northern Italy in an ultimately unsuccessful attempt to find traces of ancient Slavic settlements. He seemed more and more distanced from things Slovak, and he resided in Budapest. Given his broad view of the world, he felt constricted by Slovak patriotism, nor could he go back to it after his heady success in Prague and on the international (Slavic) scene. It has been said that he mentally lived in Slavdom, a beautiful but unrealistic fiction. After the codification of Slovak, in 1843, Kollár published a vehement attack on it, entitled *Hlasové o potřebe jednoty spisovného jazyka pro*

Čechy, Moravany a Slováky (Voice about the need for unity in the literary language for Czechs, Moravians, and Slovaks, 1846). Nevertheless, the Štúr generation continued to see him as the father of the idea of nationhood. After the revolution of 1848, Kollár was invited to Vienna, where he received an appointment as a professor of Slavic archaeology and was made an adviser to the imperial government. There, he became so estranged from things Slovak that one of his last acts was to suggest that *Slovenské noviny* (Slovak news), a paper published in Vienna, and Slovak schools should use what he called "Old Slovak," a slightly Slovakized Czech.

Ján Hollý (1785–1849)

It is tempting to say that Hollý was all that Kollár failed to be, in the sense of his understanding of the inner logic of the developments on the literary and national scenes, overlapping and interrelated as they were in the crucial first half of the nineteenth century. In him, the age of Classicism found its greatest representative. He was all the more attractive for his unassuming personality, perhaps too marked by a characteristic Slovak humility. With his tall frame, hesitant manner, and gracious smile, he earned his nickname of "gentle giant." A Russian Slavophile, Sreznevsky, went to see him in Madunice and found a saint-like man living solely for his poetry and parishioners and as poor as a church mouse.

As a student, Hollý started with the classics, penning occasional poems in Latin elegiac distichs for his professors and classmates. He studied in Skalica, Bratislava, and Trnava, where, as a student of theology, he met members of Bernolák's circle under the tutelage of Jur Palkovič, a namesake of the professor at the Lutheran lyceum. His translations of Virgil, Theocritus, Homer, Ovid, Tirteus, and Horace were collected and published by Palkovič (*Various Heroic, Elegiac, and Lyrical Poems*, 1824), as was his translation of Virgil's *Aeneid* (1828).

It was not until 1827 that Hollý started to work on his *magnum opus*, the greatest Slovak epic, *Svätopluk*, and only after the most conscientious preparation. He was clearly inspired by Šafárik's *History of Slavic Language and Literature*, in which he found the historical record of the Old Slavs, particularly the great personalities of Rastislav and Svätopluk. From his reading of Papánek, he considered the Slovaks to be the direct descendants of the heroes of the Great Moravian Empire. In this, like Fándly, he was instinctively right, long before the historians confirmed it. Six years later, *Svätopluk. Víťazná báseň ve dvanásti spevoch* (Svätopluk. A heroic poem in twelve cantos, 1833) was published in Trnava by Hollý's faithful protector and friend, Palkovič.

The effects of Hollý's heroic and national epic are hard to judge. It is clear that Štúr and his school found in Hollý what they had been missing: a great epic glorifying the Slovak kingdom. The magnificent, powerful opening sets the tone for the entire composition:

I sing of the terrible war that Svätopluk led against Charlemagne
How he, the victor, liberated himself and his
Nation from that power and became an independent ruler
And founded a great kingdom of brave Slovaks

The celebration of the founding of the Slovak kingdom is developed in a dramatic plot through the twelve cantos. The action takes place at the court of Charlemagne and in Devín, where the river Morava joins the river Danube. Svätopluk, a prisoner of Charlemagne, is released, marries Charlemagne's daughter, and is offered the rule of Rastislav's kingdom. Svätopluk arrives in the kingdom at the head of a Frankish army; when he reaches the Slovak camp, he joins it, is elected a leader, and fights against and wins over the Franks, taking control of Great Moravia. The theme of the great Slovak past is wedded to the celebration of national freedom:

Better choose glorious death and heroic suffering,
Let them cut us to pieces, spill our blood to the last drop,
Rather than bewail the lost freedom in the yoke of slavery.

This work inspired the Štúr generation; it reminded them of contemporary times, for they, like their forebears, found themselves in a time pregnant with history, when the fate of the nation was being decided. Finally, Hollý's great work, coming after Kollár's, proved to the hesitant the potential of Slovak and sped the movement toward codification of the language.

Hollý then wrote *Cyrillo-Metodiada* (1835), a religious epic about saints Cyril and Methodius, who struggled against the pagans and the Franks; the epic concludes with the solemn ordination of both brothers as bishops. The cycle of historical epics is concluded in *Slav* (1839), in six cantos, whose plot revolves around the origin of the name "Slav": Hollý shows his inventive powers as he imagines Slavdom's mythical past. However, these two epics could not compete with *Svätopluk.*

Another facet of Hollý's work, one that he would doubtless have preferred in less hectic times, was his *Selanky* (Bucolics, 1835–40). If *Svätopluk* reminded people of Homer's *Iliad,* this work was reminiscent of Virgil's *Bucolics.* In it, Hollý provides the justification for his isolated way of life:

Oh no, I wouldn't want to envy you. Just live in your city,
I prefer a modest and quiet life amidst the fields.
How pleasant it is to live in a little cottage
Sheltered by a walnut tree that reaches for the sky
and carries it over the green shade in the wind!
How before it the wild vine spreads its tentacles
And weaves near the window its fine net!
How the pure stream warbles near the marjoram and roses
As it flows straight to the neatly parted rows!

Hollý's third great interest was religious poetry, which he wrote throughout his life, and which was collected in *Katolícky spevník* (Catholic song-book, 1842).

Hollý ended his life crippled by rheumatism and blindness – the result of a fire (he survived two of them) – but he still had time to bless the efforts of Štúr, Hurban, and Hodža, when they finally codified the language in 1843. It was too late for him to make a contribution in it.

Drama and the Development of Theatre

Slovak professional theatre developed slowly. This does not mean that there was no theatre at all, but that it was not Slovak. The problem was that theatres developed in the cities and towns, and the Slovak towns were mostly German and Hungarian in language. Only during the nineteenth century did Slovaks manage to take their place in these settlements along-side the other nationalities. That Slovak theatrical life started when it did was to the credit of selfless and patriotic men such as Gašpar Fejerpataky-Belopotocký (1794–1874), a self-educated bookbinder and publisher of calendars. As a young man, he started collecting the folk-songs that Kollár later published in *Národnie zpievanky*, and during his visits to the major cities (Vienna, Budapest), he fell in love with theatre. When he returned to Liptovský Mikuláš, he started a theatre, which eventually produced thirty-three plays over thirteen years, in Slovak and Czech, as well as translations of German and French plays (Molière). The first play performed was by the outstanding Slovak playwright Ján Chalúpka (1791–1871), *Kocúrkovo, aneb Jen abychom v hanbě nezůstali* (Kocúrkovo, or we're no worse than they, 1830).

The play could not have been more relevant, as it incarnated the living reality of the very day when the audience, as the lights began to dim, focused on the stage. What the audience saw made them think about their times, with its reforms, revolutions, Slovaks writing great epics, and about trying to survive in a world where it paid to pretend that one was fluent not only in German, but also in Hungarian, which was rapidly becoming the "master's tongue." Chalúpka's comedy exploits the pretentions of the lower nobility and small-town folk and pokes fun at poorly educated, puffed-up buffoons – the prime candidates for assimilation into the Hungarian world. It also includes a Jánošík theme: in act two, students and their teacher meet a band of robbers, who feed them. *Kocúrkovo* was very popular not only in Slovakia, but also in Moravia and Bohemia. Chalúpka wrote three other plays that essentially continued the story begun in his first play.

While Chalúpka was ridiculing the beginning of the process known as Magyarization, the forcible assimilation of Slovaks (and other minorities), he was no chauvinist, as he proved with his successful farce written in Hungarian, *A ven szerelmes* (An old lover, 1835), which won him an award from the Hungarian Academy.

Chalúpka's strongest attack against the policy of denationalization, Magyarization, and chauvinism was his satirical novel *Bendegucz* (1841), written in German. It this work, several Magyarized Slovaks of the lower nobility set out, à la Don Quixote, on a quest to find their nonexistent Hungarian roots.

Karol Kuzmány (1806–66)

Kuzmány, a Lutheran pastor like Chalúpka, had the usual schooling (lyceum in Bratislava, theology in Jena). Unlike Chalúpka, however, he believed that there was a healthy basis in the Slovak nobility for a national revival. Building on the work of Kollár and Šafárik, after he settled in Banská Bystrica, Kuzmány started to realize one of his dreams: the creation of a literary journal, *Hronka* (1836–38), in which he published his poetry and prose.

Kuzmány's poetry represents the decline of classicism, but introduces a new topic: in his most important poem, *Béla* (1836), he introduces an idealized situation: a merchant who is an educated Slovak patriot is in the process of becoming engaged to Béla. The engagement – a happy and beautifully described celebation – is the content of this idyllic epic in five cantos. The Slavic element of this Slovak celebration (Svätopluk, Žižka, Peter the Great, Kosciuszko, Suvorov) is revealed in interesting dialogues, suggesting that Kuzmány's heart was in prose rather than in poetry.

Indeed, Kuzmány's *Ladislav* (1838) expresses his ideas, for which poetry was not a very suitable vehicle. His views on a variety of topics – philosophy, politics, the national movement, art – are presented in a mixture of sentimental education and travelogue. The plot is dramatic: Ladislav, an intelligent nobleman interested in ideas, falls in love with Hanka, the daughter of a pastor. Her father advises Ladislav to travel before he makes a final decision. Ladislav travels through Europe, a tour that gives Kuzmány an opportunity to introduce a philosophical theme, as well as bring in his own, Mickiewicz's, and Pushkin's poetry. When Ladislav returns, he marries Hanka, but she dies. Ladislav's Polish tutor, Luboš, becomes a hermit; his Polish friend, Konrad, goes mad (following the suppression of the Warsaw uprising); and finally, Kamilka, who always secretly loved him, enters a convent.

Kuzmány, a great connoisseur of Slavic poetry, was among the first to understand the revolutionary changes in the poetry of romanticism. He defended Karel Hynek Mácha against his detractors, and was the first popularizer of Mickiewicz and Pushkin, as exemplified by his translations.

Although both *Bela* and *Ladislav* were written in the obsolete Czech, Kuzmány, unlike Kollár, understood the logic of current linguistic development. After the revolution of 1848, he wrote a stirring hymn, *Sláva šľachetným* (*Glory to the Generous Souls,* 1848), better known to Slovaks all over the world by part of its first line: *Kto za pravdu horí*:

Kto za pravdu horí v svätej obeti,
kto za ľudstva práva život posvätí,
kto nad krivdou biednych slzu vyroní,
tomu moja pieseň slávou zazvoní.

Who burns for truth in holy sacrifice,
Who gives his life for the rights of others,
Who cries when he sees the misery of the poor,
Him my song will chime in glory.

With this poem, Kuzmány was also demonstrating his support of Štúr's Slovak. In 1849, Kuzmány became a professor of theology in Vienna; in 1860, he was a superintendent in Banská Bystrica and a fervent "Austro-Slovak" – a Slovak patriot who thought (mistakenly, as it happened) that Vienna would check Magyarization. He did not stay at his post long, as he was under constant attack by Magyar chauvinists. The last three years of his life were his most glorious: he was the vice-president of Matica slovenská, the leading Slovak cultural institution, charged with library, ethnographic, museum, publishing, and other duties connected with the preservation of the Slovak cultural heritage. (The president was Bishop Moyzes.) This example of Slovak unity – a Catholic bishop and a Lutheran superintendent – symbolized what the best of Slovaks were capable of and is treasured to this day.

5 Romanticism (1828–1871)

THE AGE OF ŠTÚR: NATIONAL REVIVAL

In Slovakia, the romantic period coincides with the appearance of the revolutionary movement of the national revival, symbolized by codification of the Slovak literary language (1843) and led by Ľudovít Štúr, as well as an armed uprising in 1848, to secure at least national autonomy from the Magyars, in which Štúr also played a leading role. The period between 1836 and 1849 was the most exciting time in the history of Slovak literature. It was truly a rebirth, a revival. Although neighbouring countries went through tremendous upheavals and their writers left very memorable works, neither in Poland, nor Hungary, nor Bohemia did these writers have to fight for the very existence of their language. But it was the lot of Slovak literature that the fight for codification of the Slovak language went on simultaneously with the fight for national emancipation.

It might seem that historical, political, and national issues would completely obscure literary ones, or that literature would be called upon to function as a vehicle for these extra-literary concerns. These were, after all, impossible times, no matter how one looks upon them. And yet, when one thinks of the great classics of Slovak literature, one thinks of Samo Chalúpka, Janko Kráľ, Andrej Sládkovič, Ján Botto, Jozef Miloslav Hurban, Ján Kalinčiak, and Samuel Tomášik, followers of Štúr. As artists they had their own ideas, but as a literary movement, they are unthinkable without Štúr. And Štúr was not simply an organizer; he was something greater.

As evidence of this, let us consider the vexing language problem, which appears so opaque to a non-Slovak. When Štúr's generation made its first public statements in the almanac *Plody* (Fruit, 1836), published in Czech on the advice of M.M. Hodža (he argued that this would demonstrate their good will toward the Czechs), the almanac was severely criticized in Prague, because nobody in Prague wrote that kind of Czech any more. The sixteenth- and seventeenth-century "biblical" Czech with Slovakisms seemed very odd indeed in Prague, where the development of language current with the Czech national revival was moving very quickly away from the putative "unity" of one or two hundred years ago. In the absence of uniformity, to odd work in "Slovak Czech" had been bearable. But no longer. In literature, the awkward use of language has a constricting influence on the quality of expression: it acts as a sort of muzzle. In *Plody*, this effect became painfully obvious; it seemed like "immature poetry." And well it might, but it was not immature, merely muzzled. This handicap aside, an unprecedented literary treasury was collected not in a century, or in decades, but in years. The years 1843–48 represent the culmination of the era of Štúr and his generation. Neither before nor since has Slovak literature produced so much, so well.

The only other movement that managed to galvanize an entire generation of poets, artists, and critics of various political and philosophical orientations – from Marxists to Franciscans – was the movement of Slovak Surrealism (1935–49), which, uncannily, arose precisely one hundred years after Štúr's generation did. Though it may be too early to pass a definitive judgement on that young and talented generation of poets, it was not without controversy, did not find ready acceptance, and cannot compare in the lasting effect it had on the national psyche. The Štúr era provided the best Slovak literature has to offer, most of it poetry. It is not that without Štúr's literary contribution the general effect of the generation would have been lessened; it is that without Štúr, it all would not have happened at all.

Ľudovít Štúr (1815–56)

At the end of 1855, Štúr accidentally shot himself in a fall during a hunting excursion. He died on January 12, 1856. This is traditionally considered one of the tragic events too painful for Slovaks to contemplate. (Another painful loss of a Slovak leader came with the death of Milan Rastislav Štefánik, without whom T.G. Masaryk might not have succeeded.) In his lifetime, Štúr accomplished the work of a dozen ordinary people. Even had he lived a long life as did his nemesis, the great Hungarian nationalist Lajos Kossuth (1802–94), he would have found himself in an increasingly desperate national situation, for, by 1894, he would not have been able to do much more than watch helplessly the mass emigration of his people to the United States and elsewhere.

The best of a great crop of young Lutheran students, a fourteen-year-old Štúr entered the literary and national history of his people when he arrived in Bratislava, in 1829, to study at the Lutheran lyceum on Convent Street. Behind him were his studies in Rab (now Györ, in Hungary), where he also learned German and Hungarian. He joined the Czecho-Slovak Literary Circle, modelling himself on his older brother, Karol Drahotín Štúr (1811–51), who wrote poetry for the circle.

Štúr started to write poetry as well. He was not drawn to theology, and so when he finished at the lyceum, he went to work as a clerk. However, he had made such an impression on Samo Chalúpka that he was called back to Bratislava to lead the Czecho-Slovak Literary Circle. It was now that Štúr began to be very active. He contacted Kollár, Jungmann, and Šafárik, corresponded with Slavic groups in Zagreb, Vienna, and Budapest, and organized the first publication of the circle's work in *Plody zboru učenců řeči československé prešpurského* (The fruits of the Pressburg groups of scholars of the Czechoslovak language, 1836). In 1836, he organized a secret meeting of sixteen members of the circle at the ruins of the Devín Castle, where they solemnly swore to devote their life to the cause of cultural enlightenment of their people. This action had something romantic about it, bridging the chasm between the ideal and real, between poetry and life. Štúr had the ability to impress young minds with the necessity for self-sacrifice for a cause in which the modern, more sceptical age no longer believed.

Štúr's interests were wide. Although history was his forte, he was also interested in philosophy, linguistics, poetry, politics, and journalism. His lectures for the circle revolved around the history of Slavs, particularly those in Russia, for whom he had developed quite a fascination, which remained with him throughout his life.

In 1837, the Hungarian authorities, who had secretly started on their program of Magyarization (following the critical comments of Kossuth, who reported from the Bratislava Land Assembly from 1832 to 1836), fully realized that such circles as Štúr's were an obstacle to their policy, and so they outlawed them. Štúr was helped by Jur Palkovič, who asked Štúr to substitute for him as a lecturer in biblical Czech, with the understanding that Štúr would continue as before. But this did not last very long, as Štúr wanted to finish his education with the usual stint in Germany – though not in Jena, but in Halle (1838–40).

From Halle, Štúr contributed poetry to a Prague magazine, *Květy* (Flowers), and he visited Prague to meet the people he so admired, with whom he had corresponded for years. He arrived in the city as someone well known and respected. Indeed, there *was* something to be respected in a man who stood poised for the greatest deeds of his life. In Halle, studying Germanic and romance cultures, he had come to understand the concept of Slavdom in a wider historical and international context, and he had returned with his mind made up: it was not realistic, or even desirable, to insist on one Slavic nation with, as Kollár suggested, "four main languages." Such a limitation was "unreal, artificial, contrary to life ... These are formulas from some books or journals, not life, so away with these dry, dead theories, away with formulas!" His first commitment would be to Slovakia and to the Slovak language. He still loved Slavs, but Slavdom, in Kollár's (and Šafárik's) sense, he now considered a fiction, a "dry, dead theory" – as he was to write a few years later, in *Nárečja slovenskuo a potreba písaňja v tomto nárečí* (Slovak dialect and the need to write in this dialect, 1846). The world "dialect," as he used it, meant "language," for Slavophiles still considered Slavdom a nation and the Slavic languages dialects.

Štúr was one of the main organizers of an unsuccessful bid to stop Magyarization with an appeal to the Austrian emperor in 1842. The failure was a very useful one, because it taught Štúr, a Lutheran, that he had to seek support among Catholic Slovaks, who were the majority. Incidentally, the Catholics continued to publish in Bernolák's Slovak (*Zora*, in which Hollý was published), since they did not suffer from the "Czech complex." The time was ripe to overcome confessional differences and act for the benefit of the entire nation. The first meeting with Catholic youths to discuss the question of literary Slovak took place in Bratislava, on February 14, 1843; the discussion focused on the suitability of the Central Slovak dialect. In the summer of that year, after securing the agreement of Michal M. Hodža, Josef M. Hurban, and the great bard Hollý himself, the problem was solved, as it turned out, definitively.

Progress was now rapid. It was as if the spring ice had broken and the stream was moving with tremendous force and speed. The following year marked the appearance the almanac *Nitra*, the first book written in the new standard literary Slovak. It was edited by Hurban and featured, among other contributors, the future greats Andrej Sládkovič, Janko Kráľ, Ján Kalinčiak, and Janko Matuška. Hurban proudly declared, "Slovak language has resurrected Slovakia." Štúr had also found time to publish, in German, a pamphlet entitled *Complaints of Slovaks of Hungary against the Illegal Actions of Hungarians* (1843). That year marked the founding of the first non-religious society, Tatrín, which mandated Štúr to compile the grammar of literary Slovak. Accordingly, in 1846 Štúr published *Náuka reči slovenskej* (Slovak grammar). He also secured a permit (after a three-years fight) to publish a newspaper, *Slovenskje Národňje Noviňi* (Slovak national newspaper, 1845–48) with a literary supplement, *Orol Tatránski* (The eagle of Tatra). A fascinating footnote to the long struggle to get the permit and to secure the paper financially was the generous support of several members of Slovak nobility (*zemänstvo*), notably Ďurko Košút, the uncle of Lajos Kossuth.

As editor of the newspaper, Štúr plunged into politics, demanding the abolition of the vestiges of feudalism in Slovak villages and insisting that education be conducted in the national language. He published, in German, another pamphlet about the Hungarian abuses, The *Nineteenth Century and Magyarism* (1845). In 1847, he was elected to the Hungarian Assembly, representing the city of Zvolen. A solemn confirmation of the correctness of his activities was the last, historic meeting of Tatrín, in 1847 in the Catholic parish of Jozef Urbanovský, in Čachtice. At this meeting, fifty-eight members (eighteen of them Catholic priests) confirmed, as representatives of the silenced Slovak nation, the choice of the Central Slovak dialect as standard literary Slovak. Most of the members had come from Liptov on a raft, down the river Váh. Commenting on this heady time, Jaroslav Vlček, the celebrated literary historiographer, said that life had never been like this in Slovakia before 1845, adding that the great struggle for the Slovak language was justified in the publication of Sládkovič's *Marína*, for "had the whole fight for Slovak brought forth nothing but this one slender book, its memory would be blessed." And then came the revolution of 1848.

A revolution is truly a ride on a tiger's back. In the midst of it nobody knows anything, as events happen everywhere in quick succession, and any attempt to take control is in vain. Štúr, as a leader, understood this to be the great chance of his life, a chance granted only once in generations. He took the chance and did his best to ride the tiger. However, this revolution, as it involved Slovakia, or Upper Hungary, as it was then known, was only a mighty and severe spasm – a delayed reaction to the vigorous and unsettling stimulation of the French Revolution and the following Napoleonic raids. Hungarian pressures led to the explosion; Slovakia provided the stage, as well as some of the actors.

Štúr welcomed the revolution, as it created the potential for action. He went to Prague to get a larger picture of the Slavic aims during this crisis in the empire, and was hailed as a great leader. In June, at the Congress of Slavs in Prague, he proposed a federal system in the Austrian Empire based on national autonomy. At this point, revolutionary events caught up with him and he took part in the Prague uprising. When it was suppressed, he went to Zagreb to secure financing for the military resistance against the Hungarians, who were making a stand against Austria and, indirectly, against the Slovaks. In September, Štúr, Hodža, and Hurban formed the Slovak National Council, which organized an expeditionary force and an uprising in the Brezová and Myjava region. They had to confront the Hungarian Guards and the Imperial Austrian Army, and against such odds they were doomed to defeat.

This failure, like the heady successes of the previous years, became one in a series of disasters: Štúr's brother Karol died, and he had to take care of his seven orphans; the newspaper was ordered closed; he was interrogated and a restriction order on his freedom of movement was imposed: he could not leave Modrá (near Bratislava) without a police permit. It was then that he wrote his last great work, *Slovanstvo a svet budúcnosti* (Slavdom and the world of the future), in German; it was published only in 1867, in a Russian translation, in Russia.

As a man of letters, Štúr began to write poetry in Czech. In *Dumky večerní* (Evening Meditations, 1836–40), his romantic temperament was revealed particularly in the mixture of beauty – the lyrical beauty of the Slovak countryside, which inspired him with ideals – and sadness, whose source was his understanding of the loneliness of his people, and of their miserable existence – a rock on which his ideals foundered. Although he wrote a number of poems in Slovak before 1848, it was only after the revolution that he returned to literature. His collection of poetry *Spevy a piesne* (Songs and lyrics, 1853) reflects the tragic situation after that fateful year.

This collection is a perfect bridge between the literature of historical epics (Kollár, Hollý) and the concerns that poetry was to take on in the future: a withdrawal from meditation on the world to meditation on the *inner* world in intimate, elegiac lyrics.

The two epics included in the collection, *Svätoboj* and *Matúš from Trenčín*, look at historical events (both of them Slovak defeats) in a new way. This was no longer a glorification of the past used to inspire the new generation, but a far-reaching look by an independent spirit who thought about history in terms of continents and millennia. Štúr was able to put these defeats in perspective and see them not as decisive, but as milestones in the inevitable historical flowering and national realization of his people.

There is a little-mentioned prophetic aspect to Štúr's contemplation of literature, particularly poetry. The only close comparison seems to be Dostoevsky's celebrated "Pushkin speech" in 1880, almost thirty yers after Štúr's work *O národných písních a pověstech plemen slovanských* (About the folk-songs and tales of Slavic tribes, 1853). Štúr stated that Slavic poetry would be the culmination of poetry as such, elevating the "Spirit of Slavdom" – expressed in the harmonic embrace of the soul and nature and resulting in the world-wide reconciliation – above anything to be found in the poetry of other nations. His faith in the salvific, almost supernatural, quality of the "word" – that is, the literary word, a feature one meets gain in Dostoevsky's "Pushkin speech" – is so strong that Štúr does not hesitate to ascribe to it an apocalyptic potential.

Finally, Štúr's historical lectures are impressive for his mastery not only of the Slavic context, but also of the history of Asia ("Asia and Europe, or the Direction of Russia in Respect to Asia," 1842), another topic dear to Dostoevsky. Štúr's early interest in things Russian also proved to be his final interest, as *Slovanstvo a svet budúcnosti* showed. He saw Russia triumphant, but with its tsarism and orthodoxy intact. In the short run, he was only partly right, but then, soaring like an eagle, he was not apt to think only in the short run.

He was a fortunate man, after all, for when he so suddently died there were other eagles soaring over the Tatra Mountains – his followers, his friends, the *Štúrovci* (Štúr's men). And they were all – if not equal to Štúr – equal to the task that the times allotted to them.

Jozef Miloslav Hurban (1817–88)

Of all the facets of Hurban's work – poetry, prose, biographies, editorial work, organizing, pamphlets, literary criticism, travelogues, active involvement in the revolution of 1848, publishing – it is difficult to choose which one takes precedence from the point of view of the history of Slovak literature. After all, Hurban, as Štúr's closest lieutenant, did all these things in assisting at the birth of something that historians later solemnly called the national revival. At such moments, something that under normal circumstances might be considered simple and unremarkable assumes great importance. And so it was with Hurban's work. However, his writing was never ordinary. Krčméry thought that in his description of Slovakia Hurban produced passages of genius. This is high praise, indeed. Hurban's prose, including his travelogues and biographies, and his publishing activity stand out.

Hurban, the son of a Lutheran pastor, subsequently became one himself, after the whirlwind of revolution deposited him, shaken but unharmed, in a little village. He had lost his parents when he was sixteen and quickly found a surrogate family in Štúr's circle. Officially, the members of the society were studying the "Czecho-Slovak language," as was incumbent upon them as future pastors of a church that used biblical Czech, but unofficially, the society was a secret brotherhood. Despite the romantic secret oath at the Devín Castle, the bonds that tied them to their commitment were emotional ones, as Štúr wanted. They were to transfer the love that a young man might have for a woman to a worthier object: the ideal of Slovakia. All of this sounds like a sort of secular nation-mysticism, and perhaps the only person who could make it seem reasonable was Štúr. He had in fact sent a beautiful girl away, telling her that he was committing his life to the cause of Slovakia. Naturally, he wanted others to do the same. For a few key years, at any rate, the commitment held.

In the five years that Hurban was a member of the circle, he tried his hand at a variety of literary genres, but his first remarkable work was written only after he had travelled to Moravia and Bohemia with the desire to strengthen the relationship between Czechs and Slovaks. Despite geographical proximity, there was not as much contact as one might assume, and each journey was an eye-opener for the young Slovak. Hurban systematically planned his visits so that he could visit the outstanding personalities of Czech life and note the social condition of the land, its industrial development, and so on. The result was *Cesta Slováka ku bratrům slovanským na Moravě a v Čechách* (A Slovak's journey to his Slavic brothers in Moravia and Bohemia, 1841), in which he developed a highly individualistic style of observation that stood him in good stead when he later described Slovakia.

He started his pastoral work in 1840 in Brezová, and it was there that he edited and published the almanac *Nitra*. His next stop was Hlboká, where he remained as pastor until his death, in 1888. It was in Hlboká that he, Štúr, and Hodža decided on the codification of Slovak in 1843, and it was where the first book in literary Slovak was born – the second year of *Nitra*. While continuing with *Nitra*, Hurban added a journal to his publishing venture, *Slovenskje pohladi na vedi, umenia a literatúru* (Slovak views on science, arts, and literature, 1846). At least in the beginning, Hurban was almost completely responsible for everything that went into the journal: he excelled as a literary critic, a defender of the new Slovak, and an author of poems, novellas, and satires. He also made a remarkable attempt to write a history of Slovak literature.

Hurban spent the revolution at Štúr's side in Prague, Zagreb, and Vienna, from where, with five hundred volunteers, he set out for Slovakia on a mission that would fail, but that would bring him honour. Thus, he was ideally placed to write Štúr's biography, which he did in the 1870s. He then returned to his literary and publishing activities and his pastoral duties. He published Sládkovič's *Detvan*, and restarted *Slovenskje pohlad'i in* 1851. After two years, he had to quit, as the authorities asked for an unreasonably high sum as a guarantee. During this period, Hurban was actively defending Slovak against the officially sanctioned Czech, and he was so vocal against Magyarization that he was fined and sentenced to jail twice. However, after the closing down of Matica slovenská and the Slovak *gymnasia*, the situation grew so desperate that Hungarian prime minister, K. Tisza, publicly stated that there was no Slovak nation. Hurban felt that the only solution was promotion of Czech-Slovak contacts, and he went back to publishing *Nitra* in Czech (1876–77).

After trying his hand at historical fiction, Hurban found his *métier* in contemporary fiction. His short novel *Prítomnosť a obrazy zo života tatranského* (Contemporary pictures from life under the Tatra Mountains, 1844) was the first fictional work written in the new Slovak. Against the background of a contrasting pair of protagonists – a Štúr-like Slovak patriot and a puffed-up Hungarian nobleman – he developed a story that actualy re-created the motivation of those who followed Štúr, along with their view of the world, while the movement was still in progress. Nor did Hurban neglect the social dimension of the time he described.

Krčméry had only the highest praise for Hurban's travelogues. *Prechádzka po považskom svete* (A walk along the Váh region, 1844), often compared to the work of Bajza and Fándly, is a powerful mixture of two strongly felt emotions: admiration for the beauty of his land and anger at those who have kept the people from developing the potential of their country. This tension propels the narrative and heightens the evocative effect of the descriptive passages.

The highest respect is usually reserved for Hurban's satirical novel *Od Silvestra do Troch kráľov* (From New Year's Eve to Epiphany, 1847). The plot is reminiscent of something that Chalúpka might have written in one of his Kocúrkovo plays: a greedy man marries a homely servant because she has won a lottery. It then transpires that she has sold her ticket and is in fact poor; the lucky winner is a young Slovak writer. Below this superficial satirical level, there is a deeper level that reveals many of Hurban's thoughts about the role of educated people in Slovakia – the nascent but poor intelligentsia, most of them recruited from the Lutheran and Catholic clergy. Hurban does not hesitate to point his finger at this group – his own flesh and blood: "Our Slovak life is handicapped mostly because until now only theologians were taking care of it. They gave us a lot of books and ideals of Slavdom, so that if the happiness of a nation were to consist of books, plans, and ideals, we Slovaks would be a very happy nation." Slovaks, he maintained, would remain in this immature state until they found a leader with a social or political agenda, someone who would rescue them from their overly idealistic, but very impractical, approach to securing their nationhood.

Interestingly, the Štúr movement did not lack men of action who combined this "practical" characteristic of the most radical kind with a lyrical disposition. This seemingly contradictory make-up was incarnated in the highest degree in the revolutionary dreamer and forerunner of Slovak surrealism, the poet Janko Kráľ.

Janko Kráľ (1822–76)

To sum up Janko Kráľ, one need only say that compared to him, Štúr was a liberal. It is true that Štúr's policies as editor of *Slovenskje Národňje Noviňi* were moderate and liberal, but this was simply the only practical way to keep this key organ of the new movement alive, after fighting for the right to publish for so many years. But Štúr was a romantic, not a liberal, politically speaking, in his literature. His aim was to express spirituality in an embrace with nature – heady stuff, and it is difficult to imagine what it actually meant. In this sense, it cannot be said that Štúr's poetry, however valued, shed much light on his own program; on the other hand, Janko Kráľ's poetry seems to have done so. Štúr, in fact, expressed the opinion, after the appearance of the issue of *Nitra* in which Kráľ had eight poems, that Kráľ was the best poet of the new Slovak.

Who was this man that he could overshadow such a colourful personality as Hurban (and, to certain extent, even Štúr), making Hurban seem positively avuncular? He did take things into his own hands in 1848: raising a mob, in several villages in the Hont region, he told all and sundry that freedom had come: freedom from labouring for the local squires, freedom to use the forests and meadows, and freedom to have their children taught in Slovak. Raising a flag with the skull and cross-bones, Kráľ and his gang marched around the district spreading the good news and taking pot shots at the mansions of the nobility. All this and much more has been said about him, but literature knows another Janko Kráľ.

Kráľ was the author of the most magical and quintessential Slovak work, the romantic ballad *Zakliata panna vo Váhu a divný Janko* (A maiden ensorcelled in the Váh and the strange Janko, 1844). In this work, Kráľ returned to the sources of both pure Slovak and the archetypal Slovak literary imagery available in the folk literature – not only the kind published by Kollár, but stories and songs he himself collected during his extensive travels in Slovakia, having understood perhaps better than any of his contemporaries what treasures they held.

In addition, he had a rare comprehension of the poetics, philosophy, and conventions of the new romantic movement. It was not just that he had made a foreign model his own, but that he had found something that was after his own heart. This is the key to understanding Kráľ and, incidentally, to understanding the strange fascination of young Slovak intellectuals between 1935 and 1949 with that exotic French import, surrealism.

Critics acknowledge the complexity of *Zakliatá panna*, which begins with the confession of a loner whose personal, intimate statement reveals a romantic, tortured soul, introducing the clues to deciphering his mystery – his native land, his childhood, and, above all, his communion with nature. The last is presented almost as a ritual purification such as that which, in traditional societies, a warrior would undertake before battle, or that which preceded the rites of passage into the perilous and lugubrious period of adulthood.

Kráľ loved Shakespeare and learned much of his work by heart. He studied Adam Mickiewicz and had an excellent knowledge of European romanticism in general, but, apart from this "bookish" romanticism, there was something in the movement that he found congenial: its glorification of the brooding loner, the outcast, the eccentric, the strange man: "strange Janko." He would wander at night, or disappear for days, sometimes even weeks or months; some said that he went as far as Bessarabia, though there is no evidence of that. He did not publish much. There are the eight poems in *Nitra*, and eleven more between 1845 and 1847, including a translation of Pushkin. But the total effect is shattering: something was born here that was larger than the movement itself. Here was new poetry, standing in the door, having arrived without knocking: not an apparition, nor the gossamer tissue of a skilful craftsman, but the eerie cry of a soul certain of its truth. Its form is an accentuated syllabic verse of twelve or eight syllables rhymed in couplets, as was the norm in folk poetry. For this reason, critics have labelled his poetry of the early 1840s "folk revolutionary romanticism."

Styled as a Jánošík-like brigand or a "brave," an outcast had a position of peculiar poignancy from which to express the existential nuances of young Lutheran students at the lyceum as they began their great nationalist adventure, which – but for the adversity of fate – might take them to the very summit, or dash them into the abyss. Štúr fed them in their nest for a while, and then they had to learn how to soar on their own. Janko Kráľ was the one who took to it right away:

> Have no roof o'er my head, have nowhere to stay,
> the lightning will show me the place where to lay.

Around me a tangle of clouds and thunder,
and I fly, fly till they tear me asunder ...
(*Orol* [Eagle])

Much of Kráľ's work was not published during his lifetime: a versified fairy-tale, three romantic stories, and three dramatic scenes in prose. Then there is his great cycle of poetry, *Dráma sveta, (Drama of the World),* a panoramic account of history, in which he issues a prophetic warning about the future coloured by the rather pessimistic attitude engendered by his revolutionary experiences. A peculiar comment expresses his mood at the time: "I was looking at the sky, looking for the angels – now I cannot find even people."

Kráľ's life, as well as the body of his work, were pieced together only in the middle of this century. Very little is known about him, and he left little correspondence. His significance is that he pioneered a new type of poetry immediately after the establishment of a new literary canon (Kollár, Hollý), creating opportunities for his successors. But he should not be credited merely for his originality, even though that would be enough to earn him immortality in Slovak letters; as well, his work set a standard that has still not been surpassed.

Andrej Sládkovič (1820–72)

If the mystery of the psyche that communicates with us in our dreams was the essence of Janko Kráľ's brooding, nostalgic evocation of the individual struggling with himself and the world, Andrej Sládkovič was his antipode. Sládkovič's work communicates peace with oneself and with the world. He abhorred rebellions, disturbances, chaos, and was the only member of Štúr's generation who earned a permanent place in Slovak literature solely on account of his celebration of the mysterious gifts of beauty and love.

Sládkovič came to Bratislava in 1840, after studying at the Banská Bystrica lyceum, where he was a member of the literary circle, which – like the one at the Bratislava lyceum – was operating in all of the Lutheran schools. His father was a teacher and an author in Krupina, and Andrej was the eighth of fourteen children. He was very poor as a student, and he supported himself by tutoring in wealthy households. He fell deeply in love with a girl he was tutoring, Maria Pischl, but her parents forced her to marry someone else while Sládkovič was in Germany finishing his theological education. The pain and suffering this caused this sensitive, quiet man was later transformed into one of the greatest Slovak love poems, *Marína* (1846). Soon afterward, he wrote his second most important long poem, a romantic epic entitled *Det-*

van, published later (1853) because of the unsettled political situation.

While Sládkovič was in Halle, a Russian friend gave him the collected works of Pushkin, whose writing he knew on the basis of a few isolated poems. Now he had access to the work that was revolutionizing Russian literature and was to inspire the great flourishing of the Russian novel from the 1840s to the 1870s. Like many *Štúrovci,* he was not immune to the charms of German philosophy, particularly those of the master of the new philosophy, Hegel. He was under the influence of Hegel's writings when he produced a dramatic-philosophical poem, *Sôvety v rodine Dušanovej* (Conversations in Dušan's family).

The Pleiad of Štúr's generation culminated in the poetry of Sládkovič. If Janko Kráľ wrote fascinating, intriguing, mysterious works, Sládkovič's writing gave a feeling of satisfaction. One lingers over his lines, hardly able to tear oneself from the verses, which many have said to be more pleasurable than those of any other Slovak poet. There is nothing artificial in the strong emotional identification that readers make with Sládkovič's poetry. He wrote his major works only when he was inspired by powerful emotion and when his identification with his subject was complete, and yet he was able to erect something permanent on his emotional foundation. The result is a lasting structure that seems to be a work of deep meditation and painstaking craftsmanship, though it was neither: when inspired, he wrote "naturally" – quickly and without much preparation.

In *Sôvety v rodine Dušanovej,* the unassuming author addresses the universal problems of the time, not simply the problems of one particular family, through the form of "conversations" in four parts. The names of the allegorical characters who take part in these conversations bespeak their roles: Dušan (Hegelian *Weltgeist*), his wife Dušica (maternal love), their son, Umko (rationality), daughters Pravduša (truth) and Vieronka (hope), their enemies Blud (lie), Strachoš (fear), and the main foe, Mefisto, the tempter and opponent of the Spirit. Athough *Sôvety* never attracted the readership of *Marína* and *Detvan,* it provides the key not only to Sládkovič's world-view, but also to the intellectual atmosphere of Štúr's generation in the 1840s, caught up as it was in enthusiasm for Hegel, which it applied to its own concrete Slovak conditions.

Marína, Sládkovič's greatest love poem, is often characterized as derivative of Kollár's *Slávy dcera.* This is a little unfair, and it diminishes the unique contribution of Marína. It is tempting to link the two poems because of the role women played in the genesis of each. In Kollár's poem, Mina symbolizes Slavdom, an abstraction derived from his meditation on the Slavs who were assimilated by the steadily encroaching Germans. However, the reader does not know for certain whether Mina (a fictionalized portrait of Kollár's wife, Friederike) is of Slavic origin, nor how reliable Kollár's meditation on the fate of those Slavs is. Finally, the concept of Slavdom that Kollár offers in the poem is not without an element of controversy that could easily be overlooked. Not so *Marína.* Instead of Slavdom, there are Slovakia, a Slovak maiden, and the easily identifiable Slovak topography. Sládkovič offers his readers a completely different world. As well, *Marína* is written in Slovak. In the Slovak language, at least, *Marína* is the greatest love poem.

In 291 stanzas of ten verses each, we are introduced to the beautiful Marína, her country, the valley of the river Hron, the author's conception of sacred love, his glorification of the beauties of the youth. Then, Marína, the evocation of the poet's unhappy love, suddenly gives way to Marína, the spirit of the Hron. The author makes clear that this is not reality, but a device to lead him to meditate upon the beauty of the region. The next step is the transformation of the love for this beautiful country into a love of life in general. Thus, the poem has a tri-partite scheme of ascending order from particular to universal. In each case, the poet identifies a sacred element, which he conceives of as a gift, and which makes life worth living.

Detvan is, in a sense, a continuation of *Marína*: formally, it has the same verse, stanza, and even rhythm. The difference is in the action and the semblance of plot in an epic story of love requited and fulfilled. There are 249 stanzas, divided into five cantos. The plot is not very developed, but the action is propelled through a series of set scenes, or images. In the first canto, "Martin," there is some drama: Martin, who is in love with Elena, has killed a royal falcon. The next canto, "Group of Friends," takes us to the archetypal Slovak setting: the *salash.* More drama is derived from Martin's liberation of Elena, who has been kidnapped by thieves. During the struggle, Martin kills one of them. "Slatina Market," the next canto, is a folk celebration with King Mathias present. As Martin confesses to the killing of the falcon (a capital offence), he also turns out to have been a hero, having killed the thief. The King rewards him with the gift of a horse. In the fourth canto, "Courting," Elena takes centre stage to play music, and among her appreciative audience is the king. The final canto, "Chase," presents the recruitment. Martin must become a soldier, but he asks to keep his Slovak costume. The king agrees.

Martin is not a hero, yet he is full of charm and, despite a certain amount of idealization, is convincingly portrayed as a simple but proud youth with whom it is easy to identify, as the reception of *Detvan* by the public proved. The society observed in this poem is Slovak, and the action takes place in a purely Slovak setting. The impression is thus that of a national epic on a grand scale. This was very important in the time of radical Magyarization.

Sládkovič's later works fall into two groups: occasional poetry and historical epic. In the latter category are works such as *Milica* (1858), using a story from the Serbian resistance to the Turks; and a retelling of the Zrínsky story, for Hungarian tradition was presenting him as a Hungarian, though he was a Slav, a Croat. Among the occasional poems are favourites when the occasion calls for the recital of a patriotic poem, such as *"Nehaňte ľud môj!"* ("Don't abuse my people!"). Finally, Sládkovič translated some plays to aid the emerging theatres: Voltaire's *Zaire*, *Socrates*, and *The Death of Caesar*, and Racine's *Phaedre*.

The body of Sládkovič's work is very impressive indeed. He tried to strike a balance between the demands of the day, in which his education, environment, philosophical training, and natural talent predominated, and the ineffable ideal of romantic poetry, which he saw so differently from Štúr and Kráľ. One might have the impression that Sládkovič was a poet of the generation that came after Štúr's, but this is not so. He belonged with Štúr. Perhaps it is because while others were waving flags, he was patiently, like a surveyor, mapping out the terrain so that he could finally show the Slovakia that everyone else was only talking about.

Samo Chalúpka (1812–83)

When Samo Chalúpka chose his epitaph, two lines from his poem *Branko* (1864), it faithfully reflected his life's main preoccupations:

> Pravde žil som, krivdu bil som –
> Verne národ môj ľúbil som.
>
> I lived for truth, fought injustice –
> Faithfully loving my nation.

In fact, it could describe all of Štúr's generation, of which Chalúpka was one of the main personalities. It was he who asked Štúr to quit his job as a clerk at the Zay Estate and return to Bratislava to take charge of the nascent movement. That Štúr acted on this suggestion reveals something about the respect that Chalúpka enjoyed.

As a poet, Chalúpka, unlike Hurban or Sládkovič, but very much like Janko Kráľ, was drawn to folk literature, particularly fairy-tales and stories of heroic personalities, thieves, and "braves." "Brave" seems to me a better rendition of the Slovak *zbojník*, who is not a simple thief. *Zbojník* contains a social dimension – such a person was idealized as a fighter against injustice, a Robin Hood. Thus, Jánošík would have been proud to be called a *zbojník*. Chalúpka thought that the Jánošík myth was the best symbol with which to awaken his nation.

After nine hundred years of inactivity, Slovak society was in a deep slumber; though some individuals were active, a few even brilliantly so, they worked on behalf of other nations. Chalúpka saw his role in the now widening national-revival movement as acting forcefully to awaken a sense of pride in his people. He rightly chose for his approach the extant folk literature, which dealt with heroes who were well known, loved, and respected. But such heroes enjoyed fame only locally. So it was with Chalúpka's best-known work, *Turčín Poničan* (*Man from Poniky Turned Turk*, 1863).

Turčín Poničan is a dramatic story preserved in the folk memory of Poniky, where a local priest found it in the form of a song and wrote it down. It is the tale of an old woman who is captured by a young Turk during the Turkish attack on Poniky and was removed to slavery. Only then does the Turk find out that the woman is his mother, from whom he was kidnapped in a Turkish raid on Poniky years before. He begs her to stay with him and his child, but she refuses, preferring to live in her homeland. Using a similar Ukrainian song as his source, Chalúpka created a masterpiece that seems to be a perfect replica – in both tone and spirit – of the folk creation. He achieved this effect by identifying himself completely with the source work, then polishing it with his poetic skill. Finally, he lifted it out of obscurity and gave it national significance. His sense of what constituted folk literature was unerring, and this was reflected in the interesting process of popular reappropriation of his work, which was spread via recitation by people who considered it folk poetry. Thus something that had emerged from folk literature returned to it.

After being schooled by his father, Chalúpka went to the lyceum in Kežmarok, where his brother, Ján, was a professor, and where he heard of Šafárik and Kollár. Upon his arrival in Bratislava, he immediately joined the Czecho-Slovak Literary Circle. In 1830–31, he was asked to lecture on Kollár's *Slávy dcera*. This was an eventful year for him. Full of enthusiasm and ideals, he rushed to Galitzia to volunteer to fight for Polish freedom in the uprising against Russia. When he arrived, the Polish cause was already suffering defeat, but he joined the action and was wounded. After he recovered from his wound, he returned to an even more active post as chairman of the literary circle (1831–32), as well as to writing. After a year in Vienna, where he finished his theological studies, he started his pastoral work. He published his first poems, which were conscious imitations of folk songs, in the 1830s; Kollár published three of them in *Folk Songs*. After this he fell silent for years, publishing only a few rather radical and stirring poems, such as *Jánošíkova náumka* (Jánošík's complaint, 1845):

> In the alpine shrub I'll make my fire
> to give the light of freedom to my Slovak family.
>
> And with the flash of my axe held in my hand
> God willing, better days will rise in our land ...

The identification of light and freedom with Jánošík's camp-fire, as well as the flash of light reflected from a sharp axe (*valaška* – a rather fancy, light axe-like weapon), are unambiguous allusions to radicalism in Chalúpka's pre-revolutionary poetry. When the revolution of 1848 broke out, Chalúpka, like many activists, went into hiding, for he was a prime target of the Hungarian Kossuth Guards. Until the end of the absolutist regime, he lay low. Then, with the restoration of parliamentary rights, in 1860, the *Štúrovci*, and Chalúpka, started to publish again. Now, he was writing heroic songs, such as *Valibuk* and *Junák* (A young brave, 1860). *Valibuk* is a fairy-tale in which good overcomes evil; though one can read into it an intention to provide encouragement to the people after the defeat of 1848, the story became a classic of children's literature because of the ease with which its rhymed verses can be memorized.

At the same time as he was composing *Turčín Poničan*, in the 1860s, Chalúpka wrote another story dealing with the Turkish incursions in Slovakia, entitled *Branko* (1864). Branko was a *zbojník* who lived a long time before Jánošík, according to the lore preserved in the Detva region. When he was reported to be near the city of Zvolen, an alarm was sounded and a man-hunt was organized, but he escaped, to be trapped near Brezno and killed. Again, Chalúpka tells the story of a hero, not a thief, in the Jánošík tradition.

The theme of freedom is celebrated in Chalúpka's best-know poem, a heroic hymn to freedom memorized by generations of Slovak students, *"Mor ho!"* (1864). The title suggests the battle cry of the ancient Slavs massacred by Roman soldiers after they refused to be enslaved. Though completely outnumbered, they attacked the Roman soldiers in a desperate act of defiance. Chalúpka found the story in Šafárik's history of Slavic language and literature. A few years later, in 1867, Matica slovenská, the only Slovak cultural institution, was ordered closed and national life was subjected to outright persecution.

Though he was to write no more, Chalúpka had provided the kind of romantic, heroic literature that would help the nation to preserve its dignity and faith in the future.

Ján Botto (1829–81)

The youngest of the four great poets of the Štúr generation, Botto is the author of the definitive literary treatment of the Jánošík myth in his heroic poem *Smrť Jánošíková* (The death of Jánošík, 1858), which Slovak critics call a "folk revolutionary romantic epic." A poet in the tradition of Chalúpka and Kráľ, Botto also drew on the inexhaustible source of folk literature. For there was something magical in the image that had already been preserved in Kráľ's *Zakliata panna vo Váhu a divný Janko* – great power, talent, and ability that was hidden in the people, lying dormant under a spell; like the maiden in the Váh, they awaited their Janko. The romantic poet was the one who could break the spell.

Unlike Kráľ, Sládkovič, and Chalúpka, Botto did not become a Lutheran pastor. He was introduced to literature in the lyceum at Levoča, where Štúr's Bratislava students found refuge after his prohibition. Thus the Levoča lyceum had a certain rebellious tradition, fortified by the activity of a Štúr disciple, Ján Francisci-Rimavský. Francisci-Rimavský urged his students to take an interest in Slovak folk literature and to collect folk-songs and -stories. Botto did so, and he also acted in the theatre, wrote poetry, which was published in the student papers, and started to read the romantic poets, among whom Mickiewicz made a particular impression on him.

At the time of the revolution of 1848, Botto was in Budapest, where he was studying to become an engineer-surveyor. He did not take part in the revolution; afterward, he finished his studies and worked as a surveyor in Martin, Banská Štiavnica, and Banská Bystrica. He opened his home to young people and introduced them to Slovak literature at a time when their schools were no longer allowed to fulfill that role.

Even in his first poems, *Povesti slovenské* (Slovak legends) and *Piesne slovenské* (Slovak songs), written in 1846, Botto showed that he understood the importance of folk literature for Slovak romanticism and the national revival. His poem *Pochod* (March, 1848), inspired by Petőfi, expressed the expectation that the year of revolutions would introduce the rule of freedom. The defeat of the Slovak cause struck a blow to his optimism, but he overcame this disappointment in *Znamä* (Flag, 1849), in which the figure of Christ comes at the time of the worst suffering to initiate the reign of justice. With his next work, *Žiaľby Svätobojove* (Svätoboj's sorrows, after 1849), Botto introduced the theme of the spell: the grandson of Rastislav calls on the soul of his grandfather to pardon Svätopluk (who imprisoned and blinded Rastislav) and thus remove the curse from the Slovak nation. In *Krížne cesty* (Crossroads, 1858), a dramatic poem, Botto dealt with shady chapters in Slovak history, such as the sadistic Countess Báthory of Čachtice, who took pleasure in murdering her female serfs, and the legendary monster Loktibrada, which impersonated accursed characters of Slovak history. Thus the appearance of *Smrť Jánošíková*, though it trod a well beaten path, was a breakthrough in the sense that fresh life was breathed into a character whom the people had chosen to represent their feelings for justice and for overcoming their penurious living conditions.

The poem is divided into nine cantos, preceded by a prologue. The first seven cantos deal with the Jánošík story, the eighth describes the origin of the Jánošík legend, and the ninth is a glorification of the Jánošik myth, elevating it to a symbolization of freedom.

Since *Smrť Jánošíkova* is a definitive literary treatment of the story of a historical personality, it is curious that Botto was not really interested in the historical Jánošík, but in the Jánošík of the folk myth. His justification for this, written in 1880, makes the following points:

> I learned about the history of Jánošík only in 1866, but what would I have done had I known about it earlier? I did not want to write a biography of the criminal tried and executed in Liptovský Svätý Mikuláš, but to portray the freedom fighter who lives in the hearts of the people and who had been growing there for the entire five hundred years of serfdom. This freedom fighter got pehaps only his name from Jánošík, and even that only partly.

Botto's point is well taken. As a romantic poet, he needed, first of all, genuine material – something that had already received the approbation of the entire people. As well, it had to be a topic that could connect the ideal of freedom to an attempt to reach for this ideal. In the age of revolution and romanticism, telling the story of Jánošík was a temptation that many poets could not resist. Only in Botto's case, however, did it find an interpreter who divined the essence of the folk-story and stayed so close to it that he did not consider it necessary to reach for the historical record.

Ján Kalinčiak (1822–71)

The great literature of Štúr's generation was poetry. Prose arrived on the literary scene later, in the second half of the nineteenth century.

Thus, both Hurban and Kalinčiak were in the minority; nor did they create a single work that could compete with the major works of Sládkovič, Kráľ, or Botto. While the folk-song helped with an easy transition of poetry into Štúr's new Slovak, folk-stories were not of similar assistance in developing a language that could reflect the quickly changing social and political scene of Slovakia. Foreign models were pointing toward the establishment of a new literary convention – realism – and the stylized Slovak folk-tales were of little help. Thus the beginnings of Slovak prose are connected with the adaptation of historical events, as was the case for poetry.

In his stories, Hurban returned to the era of Svätopluk and Great Moravia before he attempted to deal with the present. Kalinčiak worked in a similar vein: first a few historical epic poems, then stories based on legends – *Bratová ruka, Serbianka, Svätý duch* (Brother's hand, Serbian girl, holy spirit, 1845) – and finally an attempt at a historical novella – *Božkovci* (The gentlemen from Božkov, 1842). He returned to the time of "good King" Mathias, a popular ruler, for *Milkov hrob* (Milko's grave, 1845–46). In this story, Milko is fighting for the independence of the city of Žilina, when it is attacked by Ján Jiskra, from Brandýs. Milko is in love with the mayor's daughter, Maria, but Maria is loved by another man, who, in a fit of jealousy, has Milko killed. The story *Púť lásky* (Pilgrimage of love, 1846–47) is set in the era of the Turkish incursions. Janko Černok, a nobleman from Branč Castle, falls in love with Žofia, the daughter of a citizen of Myjava. They are both captured by the Turks and, after many vicissitudes, meet in captivity. Osman Aga, who also loves Žofia, learns about their love and releases them. Tragedy follows them home, when Černok, who is dressed in Turkish clothes, is killed by a peasant, who mistakes him for a Turk. Žofia dies of sorrow.

Štúr's circle considered Kalinčiak's heroes too dependent on their passions; for these characters, love was a virtual dictator, to the exclusion of all else. To respond to these objections, Kalinčiak wrote *Mládenec slovenský* (A Slovak youth, 1847). This story is set in Great Moravia, where Stanko, a young member of the Slovak brotherhood charged with preserving the freedom of Slovakia after the breakup of the empire, overcomes his passions, subordinating them to heroic action. This story had an educational function and served to support the emerging national consciousness spread by the *Štúrovci.*

Finally, in 1852, Kalinčiak was ready to attempt the first Slovak historical novel, *Knieža Liptova* (The prince of Liptov), which tells the story of King Mathias's illegitimate son, Jan, also known as the Prince of Liptov. He is fighting against the Palatine Zapoly, but because of the traitorous conduct of some of his allies his cause founders.

Kalinčiak's last work was another historical novella, *Orava* (1870). The idea came from Janko Matuška (1821–77), another follower of Štúr and the author of *Nad Tatrou sa blýska* (1851), the poem that has become the text of the Slovak national anthem. The action takes place in the seventeenth century, and the climax is the legendary "bloody wedding," when imperial troops, brought into the castle with the help of treason, captured the newlyweds, and all the prisoners were executed by beheading.

Kalinčiak's fame as a novelist rests on a work that has become a classic, which dealt with subject matter that he knew very well. It is the novel *Reštaurácia* (Electioneering, 1860), the plot of which concerns the election of the regional vice-governor, a position for which two clans of Slovak nobility compete with all means at their disposal, legal or not.

Kalinčiak was an excellent portraitist: in *Reštaurácia* he created a persuasive and memorable character in a little sketch in which the individual character is defined by the colourful language he uses. Indeed, the linguistic aspect of this novel is as responsible for its success as is its comedy. It gives a view of the Slovak lower nobility (*zemanstvo*) at a time when its death knell had been sounded, for it was being pushed out by industrialization and a fierce competition which only the higher aristocracy could survive. Kalinčiak, an opponent of the aristocracy, nevertheless did not gloat over this doomed class; in fact, over all, he paints a rather nostalgic picture.

Much of his material was taken from life, and the critics hailed *Reštaurácia* for its realistic elements. This is supported by the author's statement in a letter of July 28, 1859: "The scenes in *Reštaurácia* are from my own experience, or from stories that others told me. Everything that happens in them did take place in this or that region." Despite the obligatory "democratism" to which all *Štúrovci* had to subscribe, and despite Kalinčiak's own professed dislike of the aristocracy, a certain fondness for the *zeman* can be detected in the novel. His mother, née Ruttkay, was a *zemanka*, and was apparently a treasure trove of all kinds of interesting stories about the *zemanstvo*, particularly those of the Turiec region. The novel is packed with folk proverbs and uses very distinct language, which, Kalinčiak thought, was untranslatable. What in Slovak appears as a patchwork of styles – regional, and even individual – would become homogenized even in the best translation.

Kalinčiak was an excellent literary critic, as he showed in *Rozpomienky na Ondreja Sládkoviča* (Memories of Ondrej Sládkovič, 1847). His highly refined literary taste is particularly evident in *Reštaurácia*, for he uses none of the Štúr generation's catchwords concerning the great past or the great future of Slavs or the Slovaks. It was not that he was less emotional or dedicated than the others; it was, rather, that he realized as few did what makes a good work of art. But Kalinčiak did not experience the kind of admiration that Samuel Tomášik (1813–87) did, though Tomášik certainly was not admired for his historical prose. His *Hladomra* (1846) was a horrible story of the valley in Gemer to which many villagers fearing the Turks escaped. It was an isolated location, and most of the people starved to death. Tomášik was greeted in Prague by thousands in a great demonstration of Slavic unity on account of his song *"Hej, Slováci!,"* written to fit the melody of the Polish *"Jeszce Polska niezginela,"* which became a Slovak anthem.

THE AFTERMATH OF ROMANTICISM (1849–75)

After the national revival, which coincided with the revolution of 1848, came a period of transition. Although Sládkovič, Kráľ, Chalúpka, Botto, and Kalinčiak were still around, and some of them published their best work during this period, the movement as such had spent its force. The literature it left behind is mostly romantic and associated clearly with the heady days before 1849. The disappointment of so many hopes and the regression to an absolutist regime meant a decline in publication. The periodicals were closed and the ten-year period that followed was called "dry and dumb" by Jaroslav Vlček, a great interpreter of Slovak literature. But there is another sense in which this period can be called transitional: it was the link between the literary conventions of romanticism and realism. History itself provided the necessary impetus for this change.

Slovenské pohľady did not last very long (1851–52). From 1851 to 1859, only two almanacs were published (*Nitra*, 1853; *Concordia*, 1857). Then, in 1860, the Hungarian constitution from before 1848 was reintroduced, and a hopeful period of relaxation started. It was marked by a return of literary journals, including *Sokol* (1860–69) and *Lipa* (1860, 1862, 1864). There were also church publications, which kept the fire alive during the worst years: *Katolícke noviny* (Catholic newspaper, 1849–1905); *Cyrill a Method* (1850–70), which had a literary supplement; *Priateľ školy a literatúry* (The friend of school and literature, 1859–61); and *Cirkevné listy* (Church letters, 1863–74).

In 1861, Ján Francisci-Rimavský began publication, in Budapest, of *Pešťbudínske vedomosti* (Budapest news), and this became the paper of the Slovak nationalist movement, taking the torch from Štúr's hand. A meeting of representatives of the Slovak nation was called for June 6 and 7 in Turčiansky Svätý Martin. Six thousand answered this call, and they decided on two momentous issues: the drafting of the Memorandum of the Slovak Nation and the founding of Matica slovenská, the key Slovak national cultural institution. The memorandum demanded the recognition of the Slovak nation and a guarantee of Slovak language rights in schools and in the administration on the territory of Slovak lands (*okolie*) within the Hungarian kingdom.

The first meeting of Matica slovenská was called for August 4, 1863. Bishop Štefan Moyzes was elected president, and superintendent Karol Kuzmány vice-president. Hopes were raised by an unexpected gift of one thousand gold crowns from the emperor: it augured a better future for the Slovaks, since it meant that the emperor had put his imprimatur on the institution. Another important step in the cultural sphere was the opening of three Slovak *gymnasia,* in Revúca, Kláštor pod Znievom, and Turčiansky Svätý Martin. However, the sober voice of Ján Palárik, a Catholic priest and playwright, sounded a note of caution in the midst of the euphoria. Palárik prophetically suggested that any "deal" with Austria over the Hungarians would not work. He correctly assumed that the Slovaks were mere pawns in a larger power game being played by the Austrians and Hungarians. Rather, Palárik suggested, the Slovaks should concentrate their efforts on making some sort of accommodation with the Hungarians. It was with this intention that a political party was formed.

When the Austrian-Hungarian *Ausgleich* (changing the unitary empire of Austria, in which Hungary was one of the dependencies, into the dual empire of Austria-Hungary) was proclaimed, in 1867, Slovakia was abandoned by the Austrians, as Palárik had predicted. Consequently, Ján Bobuľa, a proponent of accommodation with Budapest, set up a party, Nová slovenská škola (New Slovak School). *Slovenské noviny* (Slovak news, 1868) became its organ. Bobuľa supported the independence of Hungary on the basis of a federal system. However, after the Hungarians were granted independence of action within their state, they decided that the Slovaks were not a separate nationality, but merely Slovak-speaking Hungarians. For next fifty years, the Hungarians were locked into a rather schizophrenic attitude of their own devising. One literary example will suffice: Kalman Mikszáth one of the most popular Hungarian authors of the period, wrote stories poking fun at Slovaks who were eager to assimilate. The high point of Mikszáth's satire was his ridicule of their Hungarian pretensions. If they did not assimilate and tried to preserve their national identity through their language and literature, they were accused of being "pan-Slavs." If they did assimilate, and said they were Hungarians exactly as the government suggested they should, they became ridiculous to Mikszáth and his readers. And Mikszáth was by no means an élitist.

In 1873, when Matica slovenská closed, what had been accomplished in its twelve years of existence? Much, it turns out. Above all, it had been the beginning of an organized national force with universal appeal. It had become a focus of much cultural activity, particularly publishing, and had attracted a new, younger generation after the *Štúrovci* began to leave. Most importantly, Turčianský Svätý Martin became an important cultural centre as a result of the founding of Matica slovenská, and this was not changed by the closure of the institution. Today, it is rightly seen as the most influential institution in the history of Slovakia. The mere twelve years of its existence were enough to accomplish the fundamental task of nation-building by integrating and focusing the energies of the emerging élite of Slovaks. By doing this, it helped to accomplish the difficult but indispensable feat of national revival.

Individuals whose youth had been connected to the flourishing of Štúr's generation also acted to prevent this period from culminating in utter devastation. Viliam Paulíny-Tóth (1826–77) was one of those enthusiastic students at the Bratislava lyceum in the 1840s. He resigned his commission of regional commissar to move to Budapest after 1860 and began publishing a political satirical journal, *Čerňokňažník* (The magus, from 1861); a year later, he began editing *Sokol* (Eagle). He was present when the memorandum was drafted and when Matica slovenská was founded. His position was explained in an essay *"Vieden či Pešt'?"* ("Vienna or Budapest?," 1872), in which he chose neither way but advocated survival and an attempt to achieve the constitutional enshrining of national rights. In defending this view, he became the most active personality during the Matica slovenská period. He was also important as a writer of fiction, particularly humorous and satirical short stories.

Ján Palárik (1822–70)

Štúr's group did not include any Catholic writers. In fact, however, it was Bernolák's group that began the movement toward standardizing the language, a position that Štúr's circle came to only after much soul-searching and after it was persuaded to accept what Bernolák's group had started. Nevertheless, there were some Catholic writers, inspired by Hollý, who wanted to continue in the great poet's tradition. Ján Palárik was one of them. In the 1840s, he not only wanted to contribute to Slovak literature, but, with the spirit of reform in the air, was quite influenced by republican ideas and wanted to apply them in his church. When he received permission to publish *Cyrill a Method*, in 1850, he used it to put out some radical proposals for church reform. He was punished, transferred to a German parish in Budapest for some ten years, and only then allowed to return to a parish in Slovakia, where he died before he was fifty.

As a playwright, Palárik started where Chalúpka ended. He revisited the humorous town Kocúrkovo, the Slovak version of *Clochemerle*, in a play called *Inkognito* (1858), with one important difference. Chalúpka had ridiculed the manners and pretensions of the inhabitants of Kocúrkovo, especially those who were embarrassed about their nationality and wanted to assimilate for pecuniary reasons. Palárik contrasted this group with the Slovaks who did not want to assimilate, building an interesting confrontation. The play has a pleasing comical charge and was very popular, playing even in Serbian theatres.

Palárik's next comedy was *Drotár* (The tinsmith, 1860). Although it was based on a foreign model, the play's characters are infused with the Slovak reality. It contrasts two brothers: one who assimilates, and one who does not. The plot is concerned with class, as well as nationality, through three characters, a nobleman, a tinsmith, and an entrepreneur, who express the changing social situation at the time; particularly interesting is the inclusion of the entrepreneur. The device of mistaken identity is used for its comical potential.

Palárik's last comedy was his most successful. *Zmierenie alebo Dobrodružstvo pri obžinkoch* (Reconciliation, or an adventure at Thanksgiving, 1862) was based on a play by the Polish author Josef Korzeniowski, but its main theme was national reconciliation between Slovaks and Hungarians. Again, the plot is based on the device of mistaken identity, and the reconciliation is that between two students: one a baron, the other an engineer. They decide to switch identifies at the same time as, unbeknownst to them, two young ladies decide to do the same. This sets off the predictable comical situations.

When Palárik decided to abandon comedy in favour of tragedy, he failed. *Dmitrij Samozvanec* (The false Dmitry, 1864), based on Karamzin's history of Russia, explores the possibilities of Russian-Polish reconciliation and the idea of individual freedom. Nevertheless, fascinating as the topic of the tragedy was, it proved too complex for Palárik.

Jonáš Záborský (1812–76)

An impressive and tragic figure, Záborský was a Lutheran pastor who converted to Catholicism. He was also a counterwright to the revivalist movement because of his oppositon to Štúr, whom he considered a demagogue who hated the *zemanstvo*. As a result, Záborský did not join in the creation of Slovak literature when the opportunity to write in Slovak occurred, but continued writing in Czech, joined Kollár in Vienna, and supported Kollár's campaign against the codification of Slovak. However, he was quite unhappy there: as the editor of *Slovenské noviny* (Slovak news), published in Kollár's "Old Slovak," he stood against developments in Slovakia – and against his bishop, who felt that Slovak literature should be written in Slovak. He left in 1852 to become a priest in Župčany, Eastern Slovakia, where he eventually died. When the period of absolutism came to an end, in 1860, he finally started to write in Slovak and soon found it so amenable that he produced a large number of impressive writings in the following ten years.

Záborský's unique, eccentric character stood him in good stead as an observer of the foibles and pretensions of his quickly changing world. Few of his writings appeared in print during his lifetime; some were published only in 1953–54. No doubt his conversion permanently estranged him from many of his Lutheran potential friends and supporters; however, what made for a very unsatisfactory social situation was a godsend for a writer-satirist. Záborský was said to possess a rational mind that made him a somewhat belated Voltairian, a satirist in the tradition of the rationalist and enlightenment authors. In fact he has been called the greatest nineteenth-century Slovak satirist.

Záborský's satirical novel *Faustiáda* is conceived as a travelogue through which Faust gets to know various countries (as well as heaven and hell). Before he goes to Kocúrkovo (which, as in Palárik's and Chalúpka's work, stands for Slovakia), Faust visits Turkey and is appalled at the suffering of the Bulgarian people. When he arrives in Kocúrkovo, he sees the entire society in satirical exaggeration. Záborský's anger was mainly aimed at the post-revolutionary situation (after 1848). The impossible situation is allegorized in *Faustiáda* in the character of Puchor. Faust blinds Puchor, Ulysses-like, and opens up the stinking barns. Nor do the heirs to the Štúr generation fare any better: Záborský paints them as hypocrites who talk about the "nation" but are as prone to selfishness as anyone else. Nor do they excel in courage: few would exchange a good career for martyrdom, or even for a good fight for their nation.

The comedy *Nájduch* (Foundling) is a necessary counterpart to Kalinčiak's *Reštaurácia*. While Kalinčiak's portrayal of *zemanstvo* uses gentle humour and the occasional ironic observation to condemn the renegade nobility who are interested only in empty pleasures and glorification of their dubious superiority, Zaborský cuts deeper. He openly, even painfully, confronts the nobility with the ordinary people whose fate it was to suffer their whims. The opening suggests the difference: a poor village girl seduced by her master, Géza Kobozy, takes the baby to its father to bring up, since she cannot afford to do so.

Géza wants to prevent a scandal and locks her up. When the people find out, they rebel and prepare to attack the manor house. The priest saves Géza, and the child stays with him as a foundling. In a parallel plot, Géza wants to run for office in an election; to get the money for his campaign, he must marry well. Here, a heroic character, Jablonkay, intercedes: he marries the heiress and wins the election. The traditional comic resolution belies the ferocity with which Záborský judged Géza Kobozy and the society that let him get away with practically anything.

In Záborský's stories is a sense of a deeply felt and suffered reality, the stuff of his own life reflected in a satirical mirror. "*Panslávisticky farár*" (Pan-Slav priest) is essentially autobiographical. "Pan-Slav" here is a word signifying the abuse a priest has to take from both civil and church authorities if he happens to have a real interest in the welfare of his parishioners. This was, in fact, Záborský's situation. The story is a bitter denunciation of the heartlessness of authorities more interested in preserving the status quo – no matter how desperate the lot of their people – than in allowing a supposed pan-Slav to act in their domain. The tactic of the authorities (secular as well as ecclesiastical) was to turn the people against their priest. In "*Dva dni v Chujave*" ("Two Days in Chujava"), Záborský contrasts the village as he knew it with a utopia, which he saw in the community of brothers and sisters, true Christians, who are concerned with each other's welfare and live as a united family, which helps them overcome their problems.

Záborský's work is still insufficiently known. *Nájduch* was staged only in 1935, and most of his plays have never been performed. As an important representative of "transitional" literature, neither romanticist nor realist, he pointed to a future that he did not live long enough to enjoy. His rhetorical flourishes and fine poetry permit us to see through the revivalist rhetoric and better appreciate what Sládkovič, Chalúpka, and Botto did.

It was not easy to survive with one's ideals intact after the disaster of 1848. Slovak patriots were often placed in an impossible situation: as citizens of the Hungarian kingdom, they identified to a great extent with Hungarian complaints against Vienna. On the other hand, they saw Vienna – however imperfect – as a natural ally against the overweening ambition of the Magyars. When the Revolution of 1848 occurred, many Slovaks welcomed it, fighting on the side of the Kossuth Guards. Other Slovaks, such as those in Štúr's volunteer army, fought the Guards and the imperial troops. It was a hopelessly confusing situation, taking its toll in broken lives, frustration, and, among a surprisingly high number of Slovak men of literature, a drastically shortened life span.

Sometimes, as was the case for Ľudovít Kubáni (1830–69), the cause of death was not political: he was stabbed to death by his brother-in-law in a dispute over a card game. He tried many different literary genres and showed great promise in all. The epic *Radzivillovna, kráľovna poľská* (Radzivillovna, the queen of Poland, 1869) is his best work. This may be because the other work for which a similar claim could be made, the historical novel *Valgatha* (1872, written in 1861), was unfinished. The novel deals with the fifteenth-century incursion by Jan Jiskra of Brandýs into Slovakia. Jiskra is opposed by Jan Hunyadi, and Kubáni takes Hunyadi's side. Politically, Kubáni was a follower of the so-called New School, which was trying to find an accommodation with the Hungarians. *Valgatha* thus presents a historical event in which Hungarians and Slovaks joined forces to fight Jiskra, an event that demonstrated their shared history and could be used to promote good relations between Slovaks and Hungarians.

Other activities started by the Štúr movement, such as the collection of folk literature, continued. Ján Francisci-Rimavský (1822–1905), considered, after Štúr and Hurban, the most important organizer of the movement, did particularly meritorious work in collecting and publishing Slovak fairy-tales, ten of which appeared in *Slovenské povesti* (Slovak legends, 1845). After Francisci-Rimavsky, August H. Škultéty (1819–85) and, more importantly, Pavol Dobšinský (1828–85), who together published *Slovenske povesti* (1858, 1880–83), did the truly outstanding task of collecting stories just in time, for oral tradition was fast disappearing and did not survive into the twentieth century.

Michal Miloslav Hodža (1811–70) was a powerful personality who drew Štúr to him with the same force as others were drawn to Štúr. A member, with Štúr, of the group that formulated and presented the 1842 complaint against Magyarization, Hodža was also with Štúr and Hurban, on their historic visit to Ján Hollý in 1843, when they decided to use the Central Slovak dialect. To support Slovak, Hodža wrote a powerful book, *Dobruo slovo Slovákom súcim na slovo* (A good word for Slovaks worthy of it, 1847). He resisted Štúr's phonetic spelling, and was the author of the etymological spelling that, with minor changes, is used today. Somewhat of a mystic, Hodža proposed a Slavic state within a monarchy during the Congress of Slavs in Prague. Needless to say, his ideas stood no chance, nor was his support of Vienna vindicated. But he could certainly find solace, such as it was, in the knowledge that he was not alone in his hopes; other worthy people, such as Záborský and Radlinský, also put their trust in Vienna.

Andrej Radlinský (1917–79), a Catholic priest, was attracted to Vienna by Ján Kollár and became the editor of *Slovenské noviny.* He also became honorary president of the Society of St Adalbert, which he founded in 1870. As well, he helped to the good word (religious and linguistic) through various publishing activities, including the journal *The Friend of School and Literature,* which he founded and edited, and its critical supplement, *Slovesnosť* (Language).

Thus, by 1875, a doubtful, even dangerous, enterprise begun by a few dreamers under the charismatic tutelage of Štúr had, over forty years, become what seemed a venerable tradition. But this was a result of the tremendous challenge taken on by men whose achievement can best be seen in the fruits of their effort. When, in 1875, the most savage national persecution started, Slovak literature and language did not wither and die. On the contrary, it blossomed and then bore fruit in the form of the greatest novelist, Martin Kukučín, and the greatest poet. Pavol Országh Hviezdoslav, that Slovak literature has so far known.

6 Realism (1871–1918)

Today, with Slovak literature flourishing, it is hard to imagine a time when a talented man did what was considered a foolhardy thing in deciding, as did Hviezdoslav and Kukučín, to write in Slovak. The language problem had been solved *internally* through codification, it is true, but why narrow one's readership? Hungarian and Czech offered themselves as real possibilities, and German was not beyond reach; yet, Slovak authors continued their almost quixotic struggle in an increasingly hostile Hungary. But they did not exist in a vacuum. The second half of the nineteenth century in Europe marked the flourishing of the realistic novel. The term "realism," like other such terms defining a certain period, can be seen as a useful descriptive aid without necessarily having any prescriptive value. Great novels were written in England, France, and Russia. The Russian influence, in particular, made itself known in the work of contemporary Slovak novelists. This is partly because of a similarity of context. With the exception of Dostoevsky, most of the great Russian novels are stories that take place in the countryside, not the city.

One thinks, first, of Turgenev and his *Hunters' Sketches, Fathers and Sons,* and *The Nest of Gentlefolk.* He would be temperamentally closer to Slovak novelists than would be, say, Dickens or Balzac, with their primarily urban concerns. Slovaks did not then have a metropolis, and they still do not have one. Bratislava has a population of about half a million today. A century ago, it contained fewer than two hundred thousand people, most of them Hungarian and German. Other cities were slowly becoming Slovakized, but only one, Turčianský Svätý Martin, was considered purely Slovak. Thus, the rural orientation of Slovak literature was preserved well into the twentieth century, and the last truly rural novels were written in the 1930s.

Conditions for Slovak writers between 1875 and 1918 were appalling. Writers such as Seton-Watson and Björnsterne Björnson provide a clear, objective record of this sad time of forced Magyarization and the mass exodus of Slovaks to the United States, Canada, and elsewhere. Soon, more Slovaks were living abroad than in Slovakia. In the context of such discriminatory Hungarian practices as allowing only a tiny percentage of university students to come from Slovakia, there was a resurgence of interest in co-operation with the Czechs, and in leaving Hungary to study in Prague (where students from Slovakia founded a society called Detvan – literally, "man from Detva," a region in central Slovakia, and reminiscent of Sládkovič's eponymous poem) or Vienna. Some Lutheran students continued with their traditional stint at a German university. One of the main representatives of this period, Svetozár Hurban-Vajanský, studied at a German gymnasium.

Svetozár Hurban-Vajanský (1847–1916)

A son of Jozef Miloslav Hurban, Svetozár Hurban took the pseudonym "Vajanský" at the suggestion of Viliam Paulíny-Tóth. Following in the literary foosteps of his father, he did much for Slovak prose, which, after the period of romanticism, clearly needed to catch up with poetry. Vajanský edited *Slovenské pohľady* (1881–90), as well as *Národné noviny* (National news, 1878–1914), in Turčianský Svätý Martin, where he went after he became disillusioned with his law career. Even more than his father, Vajanský built an impressive reputation, and his ideas, right or wrong, had to be respected. He developed good relations with leading Russian Slavophiles, including I.S. Aksakov and V.I. Lamansky, and wrote critical studies of Turgenev and Tolstoy, one of which was published in Russia: *"Graf L. N. Tolstoy kak khudozhnik i mudrets"* (*Slavyanskoe obozrenie,* 1892). A conservative and deeply religous, even mystical, thinker in the tradition of his father, Vajanský was never afraid to make a statement in defence of his nation and its rights, and he was imprisoned three times for his protest against forced Magyarization. Although he spent most of his life in Turčiansky Svätý Martin, he witnessed the Prussian war as a student and took part in the occupation of Bosnia and Herzegovina as a Hungarian soldier. His family background, education, travels, and considerable talent made him, next to Kukučín, who was thirteen years younger, the most important nineteenth-century Slovak novelist.

Vajanský's first mature literary statement, which marked a new poetic age and made his name as an important author, was a collection of poetry entitled *Tatry a more* (The Tatras and the sea, 1879). It contained echoes of the poetic concerns that dominated the Štúr period; for instance, "Ratmír" is based on a historical incident from the times of Matúš Čák Trenčiansky (d. 1321), one of the romantics' favourite periods. However, much of the collection, which is divided into seven cycles – "Sounds," "Lighthouse," "Adriatic Letters," "Dreams and Legends," "Ratmír," "Herod," and "Echoes" – expresses realistic concerns and contemplates the future of Slavdom. The mixture of styles, approaches, and imagery foreshadows most of the author's future concerns. The striking immediacy in the "Adriatic Letters" cycle derives from Vajanský's personal experience as a soldier in Bosnia and Herzegovina, whose people he admired, but whom, serving a hated power, he actually helped to enslave. He resolves this quandary by pondering the historic role of Russia, which had just helped to liberate Bulgaria from Turkish rule. This action was considered by Vajanský to be a harbinger of a glorious Slavic future. The influence of his Slavophile friends and N.J. Danilevsky's *Russia and Europe* may have contributed to this attitude. The one forced note of the collection comes in "Herod," in which his emotional over involvement devalues the artistic attempt: two Slovak orphans are taken away from Slovakia to Hungarian regions, where they will grow up Hungarian. On the other hand, a breath of fresh air in the collection is its novel poetic statement, unencumbered by much of the older concerns: what had previously been treated in a pathetic, romantic tone is suddenly accepted.

Vajanský's next collection of poetry, *Spod jarma* (From under the yoke, 1884), is also concerned with the tragic situation and emigration of the Slovak people. Because of its sharply critical content, was the collection published in Prague. Even his last collection, *Verše* (Verses, 1890), shows how difficult it was not to think about the national situation. Yet, the poetry in this volume is saved by a redoubled concentration on form; the experimental character of much of this collection saves it from the desperation of such cycles as "From Gloomy Moments," which opens the collection. It is as if Vajanský was trying to prove that the Slovak language was flexible enough to permit a wide range of poetic expression.

If the great promise of his first collection of poetry was never realized by the subsequent collections, Vajanský still managed to break away from romanticism and open the door for the new poets. There are poems of genius in *Spod jarma,* and his substantial talent can be seen even through the most partisan of diatribes. He also continued to improve technically, and such formal improvements were a substantial contribution to Slovak poetry.

Vajanský's prose developed differently. When, after a few rather good stories, he published *Duchovia sudov* (The spirits of the casks, a short novel, the reaction of readers and critics alike was indifference. But he continued to write, and he was particularly fruitful between 1880 and 1883, when he produced short stories – *"Podrost"* and *"Kandidát"* (Underbrush, Candidate), in 1881, and *"Búrka v zátiší," "V malom meste,"* and *"Dve sestry"* (Storm in the shelter, In a small town, Two sisters), in 1882 – novellas – *L'alia* (Lilly, 1880) and *Letiace tiene* (Flying shadows, 1883) – and a novel, *Suchá ratolest'* (A dry branch, 1884). These works quite matter-of-factly deal with contemporary problems and show an activist Slovak character, as if to compensate for the somewhat depressing outpourings of his previous two collections of poetry.

In Letiace tiene, Vajanský captures the last years of decline of the *zemanstvo.* It seems that the protagonist, landowner Imrich Jablonský from Jablonové, has successfully mastered the transition to the present: through marriage and shrewd financial investments, he has managed to accrue quite a fortune. It seems a waste of time to continue working on his estate; instead, he concentrates on his financial career, trying to advance it with the help of Bauer, his distant relative and a German speculator, and Zweigental, a Jewish money-lender. The result is a financial disaster from which he manages to extricate himself with the help of a Slovak, Eugen Dušan. Clearly, Vajanský was advancing his own ideals in this novel, which begs the question, How realistic is his realism?

Vajanský sees Jablonský's attempt to escape from the land as fatally flawed: it is the cause of his downfall. Instead, Vajanský implies, Jablonský should have cultivated his estate and worked for the good of his nation. It was, after all, a Slovak who helped him out. Dependence on foreigners, represented by Bauer and Zweigental, leads to trouble, for they have only their own interests, not those of Slovaks, in mind. Vajanský suggests an alliance of the *zemanstvo* with the new, emergent Slovak intelligentsia as a solution. Yet, the novel is anchored in Slovak reality as seen and felt intimately by someone who made it his life's business to stay attuned to the cries and whispers of his nation. Vajanský infused with his idealism a work whose realistic framework makes it a respectable attempt at a novel in the grand tradition of the Russian masters.

Vajanský's next work, usually considered his best, *Suchá ratolest'* (1884), also deals with the Slovakia of the 1870s. However, it is a much subtler work than *Letiace tiene.* Officially (according to the Magyar position), Slovaks did not exist, in the earlier work it had been important for Vajanský to remind his people not only that they existed, but that they could survive even on their own (native) resources. *Suchá ratolesť* adapts the concepts of the symposium and the *Bildungsroman*. The protagonist, Stanislav Rudopolský, returns home from a long stay abroad. In his village, Rudopolie, he meets a group of people who affect him in various ways: Adela influences him erotically, Maria Vanavská, erotically and morally; Vanovský, morally and ideologically; and Tichý, morally and nationally (see Števček, *Esej o slovenskom románe*, p. 84). Rudopolský returns to Slovakia with his eyes wide open, his mind a *tabula rasa*, and his attitude an enthusiastic desire to learn. Simultaneously, an inner process of working out the national consciousness and emotional growth is quietly accomplished.

The rebirth of Rudopolský may be criticized as an example of the idealistic and unrealistic Vajanský ignoring the evidence of his senses. But Vajanský was also a religious writer and something of a mystic. He would have been the first to admit that Rudopolský did not represent a majority of *zemanstvo*, who would have been unlikely to experience a metanoia, a radical turn, such as Rudopolský did. After all, Rudopolský says, "Nobody can stop the decline caused by individual sin ... But does that mean that individuals like myself cannot come forth?" With this in mind, it is hard to accuse Vajanský of being a reactionary, as some radicals of the time, writing from Prague, did. In fact, Vajanský's contemporary readers were thankful for what they thought was a realistic image of their Slovakia. They could also appreciate the maturity and high artistic standards of a novel that matched some of Vajanský's great inspirations: the works of Ivan Goncharov and Ivan Turgenev. Not the least important of his accomplishments was the development of a very polished conversational prose style. Here, he was clearly a pioneer, although it sometimes seemed he forgot that his characters should be more than mere devices to advance his philosophy – often they spoke and thought just like he did. But this is not a major concern; if it is a flaw, he shares it with the likes of Dostoevsky.

When Vajanský returned to the topic of the relationship between landowners, the intelligentsia, and businessmen, in *Koreň a výhonky* (The root and the shoots, 1895–96), he sounded a warning: if the shoots leave the root (tradition, the family, the nation), they perish. The life-giving powers of the nation were now represented not by the *zemanstvo*, but by the common people. Ján Drevanský becomes estranged from his roots and perishes, while Mirko Kladný, slowly returns to his roots.

Vajanský's longest novel, *Kotlín* (1901), was written in prison, where the Magyar authorities sent him because of his outspoken journalism.

Though this work throws a very interesting light on some of the most acute problems of the day, particularly an emerging split in the Slovak intellectual movement between representatives of the young generation and traditionalists like himself, it fails as a novel. The story of a doomed *zeman*, Andrej Lutišič, who ends his own life, concludes Vajanský's explorations of the possibilities that this class had for the revival of the national aspirations of the Slovak people.

Vajanský's other activities – as journalist, memoirist, writer of travelogues, and literary critic – made him the most resourceful and well-rounded author of his time. The younger generation rejected not his tireless work of more than four decades on behalf of his nation, for which he paid with imprisonments, but his idealism, his orientation toward the Russian monarchy, and his conservatism. Whatever his faults, however, he was not doctrinaire, as were many of his critics. Unlike them, he created something new, the Slovak social novel, opening the way for Kukučín, Maróthy-Šoltésová, Vansová, and others. It is to him, as well as to Hviezdoslav and Kukučín, whom we turn for examples of solid, mature, and, in many senses, permanent achievement: these are the classics of Slovak literature.

Pavol Országh-Hviezdoslav (1849–1921)

Orava, a poor mountainous region of Slovakia – and one of its most beautiful – gave Slovak literature many writers and poets, though none greater than Hviezdoslav. And yet, Hviezdoslav could have become a Hungarian, or even a German, poet. As a child, he was in love with poetry before he fell in love with a language. By the time he was fifteen, in 1865, and studying in Miskolc, Országh (Hviezdoslav is a pseudonym chosen in 1875, meaning "the one who glorifies the stars,") had a notebook full of poems in Hungarian and German, including "Der grosste Schatz" and "Die Lebens-Bahn." His dilemma was that he loved Hungarian poetry, but felt that he was Slovak. He learned about Hungarian and world poetry before he discovered the Slovak poetry of Kollár, Chalúpka, and Sládkovič. Although some Oravian friends sent him Slovak poetry when he was in Kežmarok, he had to make his own decision. When he made it, Slovak literature gained a poet whose work is not only a fitting complement to Sládkovič's, but is one of the best that Štúr's generation created.

Even before he graduated from the *gymnasium*, Hviezdoslav published a collection of poetry, *Básnické prviesenky Jozefa Zbránskeho* (Poetic spring flowers of Jozef Zbránsky, 1868). This collection shows the heavy influence of Sládkovič and features some sentimental celebrations of the beauties of Orava, while also suggesting a mature determination and understanding of the role of the poet in his nation. It is the best evidence of the successful solution of his dilemma.

When he enrolled in the Prešov Academy, Hviezdoslav found a good friend in an enthusiastic poet, Koloman Banšell (1850–87), with whom he published, in 1871, an almanac of young writers entitled *Napred* (Forward), whose significance for Slovak literature was a move away from the elevated poetry of the *Štúrovci* toward realism. The thirteen poems that Hviezdoslav contributed, reflective ruminations on the mystery of existence, showed tremendous evolution toward a more subjective poetry. The almanac was criticized by Jozef Hurban, who resented its departure from the agenda of the *Štúrovci* and did not realize that the young poets were struggling to find their own means of expression. Following the criticism, the pages of the few journals left were suddently inhospitable to the group of young poets. A period of trial and search began anew, culminating for Hviezdoslav in the publication of collection entitled *Jesenné zvuky* (Autumn sounds, 1878).

Hviezdoslav's name was well chosen. In the 1870s, he truly was a star child: the decade was dominated by his poetry of cosmic reflection and meditation, suggesting a certain tension between what he conceived as idealistic and realistic attitudes toward his existence. His realistic poetry appeared for the first time in the collections *Oblaky* (Clouds, 1879) and *Krb a vatra* (Hearth and camp fire, 1880). *Oblaky* is a cycle in which he takes a philosophical view of some of the most disturbing recent events, such as the oppression of Slovakia in 1867. The clouds, as cosmic messengers, recount what they have seen on earth. Injustice is not treated in the manner of Chalúpka, or Botto, but in a contemplation of the true values of humankind and how they are applied or distorted in his day. *Krb a vatra*, which was not published in the poet's lifetime, documents the universal dilemma of how to resolve the tension between private and public life and the different responsibilities they entail. It was perhaps here that his concentration on family life, as opposed to public life, suggested an orientation closer to a view rooted in the consciousness of his people – the traditional life, which became the source of his later world-view.

Hviezdoslav's life was relatively uneventful, compared to those of the poets in the romantic era. In the 1870s, he established himself in the legal profession. He got married, and soon thereafter suffered a great loss when his beloved sister died. In 1879, he left Dolný Kubín for Námestovo, where over the next twenty years he created almost all of his substantial poetic *oeuvre*. It was in the 1880s that he wrote the poetic composition with which his name is most often associated, *Hájniková žena* (Gamekeeper's wife, 1884–86).

Hviezdoslav's cycles of poems, whether lyrical or epic in genre, always have a certain inner unity; they reflect a basic philosophical and spiritual disposition permeating his compositions. In the cycle *Sonety* (Sonnets, 1882–86), he does not abandon his cardinal religious understanding of existence but continues the movement that he began in the 1870s, a movement "from the stars to the earth":

> But, let's climb down from heaven,
> it would be better to enter into oneself;
> the virtue resides in concentration.
> There is no standpoint in thin mists,
> of all the stars only earth is near
> and here's enough of the great work to be done.

Of the lyric cycles, the most extensive is *Letorosty* (Growth rings, 1885–96), which is in fact an intimate record of the poet's state of mind during his most creative period, when he was wracked by serious doubts about the impact of his poetry on his nation, and about what level of understanding of his poetry his society was capable of. *Letorosty* also contains poems in which he comments on the painful losses of his and his wife's parents and of his brother, which lead him to reflect on the merciless march of time and quickly encroaching old age. He is drawing up a balance sheet, but instead of surrendering to resignation and pessimism, he resolves to work even harder for his nation. More and more, he sees his poetic work in terms of a mission. He applies this concept even in a moral sense and often acts as a judge or a prophet in his poetry, assessing the sins and moral decline of his times. Only spring time and youth are guarantors of better times ahead. He sees the present generation as lost: they are either victims or victimizers. This vicious cycle can be broken only by the next generation.

Hviezdoslav was equally at home with the epic poem. His works in this genre are often described as "lyric-epic," because they contain long, lyrical passages in which he creates a general framework or background featuring sensitive descriptions of nature. This is not, however, nature in a pseudo-classical stylization, but with Hviezdoslav's instantly recognizable signature (see Krčméry). His visual evocation of identifiably Oravian natural surroundings was new to Slovak poetry, and is one of his most attractive and oft-imitated traits.

Three epic compositions were written during Hviezdoslav's stay in Námestovo: *Hájniková žena, Ežo Vlkolinsky* (1890), and *Gábor Vlkolinský* (1897–99). Of the three, *Hájniková žena* is considered the culmination of the poet's mature period.

The story of Hájniková žena is simple: into the ordinary life of the gamekeeper, Michal Čajka, and his wife, Hanka, comes tragedy, in the person of the decadent nobleman Artuš Villáni, who tries to seduce Hanka. To defend her honour, Hanka kills Villáni. Hviezdoslav's keen psychological insight into Hanka's mind in both happiness and tragedy is his highest achievement. He returned to these characters in "Two Visits" to provide an epilogue that ends on a happier note.

Hájniková žena uses octosyllabic and nonosyllabic iambic verse with a rich variation in rhyming scheme, enlivened by the interpolation of songs with a trochaic or dactylo-trochaic verse. Compositionally, most of the integrating elements are connected to the three main characters, who are sensitively delineated and individualized: Michal, a confident man with a temper, but also a man of rare honesty and integrity; Hanka, faithful and kind, but also capricious; and the amoral Villáni, whose decadence is the result of an uncontrolled, and perhaps uncontrollable, egoism. The repeated use of three leitmotifs, the cottage, the mansion, and the maple, supplies a kind of poetic shorthand for expression of some of the more difficult emotions. The cottage represents the common folk; the mansion serves as a symbol of artificiality; the maple is a symbol of the life within and of nature. The inclusion of authorial reflection and the interpolation of songs, both highly functional devices, heighten the tension, rather than merely delaying the action. And, as in nature, the mysterious force of regeneration overcomes even the deepest of tragedies. The conflict between the mansion and the gamekeeper's cottage bears the remnants of romantic treatment and the author's idealism. The desirability of regeneration of Slovak society was also present in *Ežo Vlkolinský*, and *Gábor Vlkolinský*, in which romanticizing treatment gives way to realism.

The *zemanstvo* inspired Hviezdoslav with its potential to revive the depressed fortune of the Slovak people. This coincidence of attitudes toward *zemanstvo* between Vajanský and Hviezdoslav points to some truth behind their hopes. Although today's "progressive" critics poke fun at the "inevitable" decline of this class, artists of the stature of Vajanský and Hviezdoslav took the Slovak gentry seriously. When Hviezdoslav wrote his epics about the depressed *zemanstvo*, his intention was not to sound their death-knell, as is often thought, but to inspire their regeneration.

In *Ežo Vlkolinský*, Hviezdoslav portrays a *zeman* family, the Vlkolinskýs, whose son, Ežo, decides to marry Žofka Bockovie, a simple peasant girl. Ežo's mother, Ester, cannot agree to this match for dynastic reasons: the family's fortunes have long been in decline. By marrying below his class, Ežo will further drag the family down, and their hopes for the future will disappear. Ežo has to leave home, and he finds refuge at his uncle Eliáš's house. After the wedding and the birth of a child comes a family reconciliation, achieved through the agency of the grandson. Hviezdoslav was an excellent observer of the *zemanstvo*, whose behavioural and linguistic mannerisms he documented with almost a historian's penchant for accuracy. Of great interest today are the ceremonies of carnival season (*fašiangy*), courtship, and marriage. The conclusion of the poem suggests a solution to the problem of the *zemanstvo*, which Hviezdoslav saw in the unity of this class with the common people.

Gábor Vlkolinský takes this line of thought further, portraying the end of the line for the irresponsible gentry. The Vlkolinskýs run down their estate to the extent that their son Gábor, a good, kind young man who searches for, but cannot find, love, must go to live with a peasant family. There is little hope of rebuilding the once wealthy estate. Hviezdoslav returned to the stories of Ežo and Gábor in "Two Visits."

The poet gave much thought to spirituality, and his own contemplation of the religious heritage of the Bible gave rise to a constant stream of poems. One of the longer cycles is *Žalmy a hymny* (Psalms and hymns, 1885–95), a kind of spiritual diary detailing the doubts, meditations, polemics of a man living in a century that wanted to exclude God from life. The strong faith of the poet is locked in a struggle with the spirit of the times; while he turns polemically both to the world and to God in a way unprecedented in Slovak poetry, it is with the humility of one who seeks understanding. In *Agar* (1882), *Rachel* (1892), and *Christmas* (1897), he connects biblical themes to the painful problems of the day. But nowhere is he as innovative and as comfortable as in his lyrical cycles of nature, *Prechádzky jarom* (Spring walks) and *Prechádzky letom* (Summer walks), both written in 1898.

Hviezdoslav is at home with nature, which he anthropomorphizes into a kind of companion. Nature also reflects God, who is present in the sun (the "eye of God") and can see the natural and human worlds as one. It is contact with nature – ever-changing yet constant in its regenerative pattern – that reminds the poet of his age:

I, an old man, leaving
my modest little abode
for exquisite nature
was a little terrified
when I thought: really,
what sort of welcome will they give me
out there ... ?

A number of Hviezdoslav's shorter epic poems are a fitting complement to his longer ones, because they deal with a plethora of issues and problems not addressed elsewhere. The psychology of the Slovak peasant is explored in *Bútora a Čútora* (Bútora and Čútora, 1888); the charm of pure, gentle love is the theme of *Prvý záprah* (The first team, 1898); freedom, unity with nature, the role of popular fantasy, and the charm of youth run through *Na obnòcke* (An overnight pasture, 1889).

Hviezdoslav made an important contribution to Slovak drama as well. One of his plays, *Herodes a Herodias* (Herod and Herodias, 1909), represents the best attempt at Slovak drama before 1918. The story of Herod Antipas and his relationship with Herodias, Salome, and John the Baptist serves as the background for penetrating characterizations and great philosophical depth. Unfortunately, what stood Hviezdoslav in such good stead in the rest of his literary work – his relative physical isolation from major cultural centres – led to weakness in his use of the dramatic form. He lacked frequent contact with good theatre, and this showed in play's cumbersomeness and technical flaws. A slightly adapted version of the play was staged for the first time only after Hviezdoslav's death, in 1925, after which it passed into the repertory of the Slovak National Theatre.

His translations are among the treasures of Slovak literature. He translated the greatest works of Shakespeare, Goethe, Schiller, Mickiewicz, Słowacki, Lermontov, Pushkin, Madách, and Petöfi. For example, he translated Pushkin's *Boris Godunov, the Prisoner of Caucasus, Gypsies,* and other poems.

Hviezdoslav's importance for Slovak literature in general stems from his role as a synthesizer of the valuable heritage of early-nineteenth-century poetry, which he adapted in such a discriminating manner that the improvements and accomplishments of his predecessors found their application in his poetry. In addition, he enriched Slovak poetry with words taken from other languages, and with neologisms, which passed into the common Slovak poetic vocabulary. His translations proved to expressive quality of Slovak, demonstrating the language's ability to communicate even the most subtle artistic expression. Technically, he was a pioneer of the new, accentuated, syllabotonic verse, which he built on an iambic foundation, often using rhythmic-syntactic divergence, characteristically omitting caesura and rhythmic-syntactic parallelism.

Finally, Hviezdoslav had the enviable fate of living long enough to see thc end of the national oppression, and to receive accolades from the government of the new Czecho-Slovak Republic after 1918. He was finally able to publish *Krvavé sonety* (Bloody sonnets, 1919), a collection of poetry written in 1914 in which he angrily reacted to the war. The government awarded him a life pension, and in exchange he became an "official poet," whose copyrights were transferred to the government. After writing some pro-government propagandistic poetry, he began to have doubts, which he expressed in the poem *Na pamäť stých narodenín Andreja Sládkoviča* (In memory of the one-hundredth anniversary of the birth of Andrej Sládkovič, 1920).

Martin Kukučín (1860–1928)

It was Kukučín's fate to leave his country, as did countless poor Slovaks who sought survival overseas. When he returned, he found his homeland more of a foster parent than a real one and had to leave again. Thus, he stands in the history of Slovak literature as a painful reminder of uncomfortable truths, as a man of integrity who would, at the end of his life, rather retire abroad than make a compromise against his conscience. To this day, it is not clear whether Slovak literature has had a better prose writer.

To be born in a simple peasant's house in Jasenová, in the region of Orava, as was Matej Bencúr (Martin Kukučín is a pseudonym), was not all that unusual; few Slovak writers were born to families of fortune and leisure. But Kukučín, as a writer, quickly managed to turn his humble background into a literary commodity. Even Vajanský, whose novels were peopled with the fast-disappearing *zemanstvo,* saw the value in Kukučín's work. Kukučín's village stories are fine psychological portraits of highly individualized human beings whose emotions, failures, and little victories are observed not by some detached and objective scientist, but by someone who could identify with them and see their life from the inside. In some of his best stories, such as *"Neprebudený"* (The unawakened, 1886), his readers did not care that there was very little plot or that some other formal requirement may have been missing, for they would be caught up by his gift for creating a special atmosphere.

The first period of Kukučín literary work, in the early 1880s, was spent searching for his own form of literary expression. In 1885, there was a sudden and decisive change in his plans. Though he wanted to study theology, he was estranged by the anti-Slovak feeling in Bratislava and decided instead to study medicine in Prague, where he went with Dušan Makovický, who later became famous as Lev Tolstoy's last doctor. He stayed in Prague from 1885 to 1893, contributing stories to Slovak journals, calendars, and such, and taking an active part in Detvan.

He arrived in Prague as a mature writer with three strong stories to his credit: *"Rysavá jalovica"* (Red cow, 1885), *"O Michale"* (Michaelmas, 1886), and *"Neprebudený."* The last story stands out. Its protagonist is

Ondráš Machul'a, a gentle, physically mature but mentally and emotionally retarded village boy employed as a gooseherd. When Zuzka Bežan tells him, just for fun, that she would like to marry him, Ondráš takes her at her word and ponders how to get decent clothes for the wedding: "The hardest thing of all is to get the new suit; after that, the wedding is easy ..." For the simple-minded youth, this is the biggest obstacle to his happiness.

We see Ondráš's worries from the inside. As his imaginary preparation for the wedding continues, Zuzka is also getting ready for a wedding, but to another young man. The tragic dénouement of the story takes place during the wedding, when there is a fire in the barn in which Zuzka's geese are kept. Ondráš rushes in to save them and perishes in the flames.

Nothing that Kukučín wrote before or after had as powerful a tragic and pathetic force. Ondráš's psychological motivation and the persuasive description of his guileless, defenceless, humble status make it almost unbearably painful reading. Nor can Zuzka be really blamed for his death, for her teasing does not overstep the bounds of the kind of ridicule that the village idiot would normally receive. It is precisely for this reason that the waste of a human life makes such an impact – we know Ondráš and sense his fragile, even beautiful nature; his guilelessness is in fact spiritual purity. Thus his death has an inner logic too, as he is too good for this world. This is a considerable accomplishment for an author in his mid-twenties.

His stay in Prague introduced Kukučín into a busy and culturally rich life. The new literary and artistic influences that came from his reading and his visits to the theatres were digested and discussed during the meetings of Detvan, where he would give reports on Czech and Russian literature. Simultaneous with this artistic growth, however, came the realization that the soil on which his talent fed was becoming more distant. His keen feeling of uprootedness and estrangement from his native land found expression in a number of stories, such as *"Na obecnom salaši"* (At a public *salash*, 1887).

Kukučín drew on his early experiences, despite his growing awareness that the loss of contact with his homeland might have unpleasant consequences, creating during this period a work infused with a pleasant, carefree atmosphere, *Mladé letá* (The early years, 1889). A short novel about student life in a *gymnasium*, it is the most significant of an entire cycle of writings devoted to this theme. Through the conflict between students, Ferko and Miško, who vie for the attention of the beautiful Elena, Kukučín introduces us to those happy times. The evocation of young love and the comical misunderstandings caused by the rival's attempts to hide their true feelings contribute to the impression that Kukučín himself, as his biographers confirm, experienced much joy during these days. Yet, even here he brings in a wider and more serious context: the relationship of the educated to the simple, poor people. Like the best Slovak writers, he had a genuine desire to help the people, but he realized that such ideals could lead to a condescending attitude. He knew that the simple people, no matter how uneducated, possessed a certain dignity and qualities that often raised them above the more fortunate and better educated.

Stories from Kukučín's Prague period included his contribution to the literary debate about the merits of *zemanstvo*, a subject that no writer of the period could ignore. In *"Keď báčik z Chochoľova umrie ..."* (When my uncle from Chochol'ovo dies ..., 1890), he contrasts a *zeman*, Aduš Domanický, with a merchant, Ondrej Tráva. While Domanický is a buffoon given to painful exaggeration, Tráva is a former peasant who wants to succeed by buying low and selling high. In fateful encounter in a market, Tráva's greed confronts the unscrupulousness of the impoverished *zeman* Domanický, who pretends that he has some grain to sell. The price seems very advantageous to Tráva, so he "buys" and gives Domanický the down payment. There is, of course, no grain. The only hope that Domanický has for improving his fortunes is the anticipated death of his wealthy relative from Chochol'ovo. The most significant characteristic of the decadent *zemanstvo* is captured here: a refusal to see that the only way out of poverty is hard work. One is reminded of Chekhov's *The Cherry Orchard* (1904), in which the nobility facing bankruptcy do not want even to hear of practical solutions to their problems, but instead pin their hopes on a similar inheritance. This is a conflict between the refusal to face reality (Domanický) and the willingness to believe in a reality that is revealed to be nothing but a sham (Tráva). Eventually, after his uncle dies, Domanický returns the money to Tráva.

Greed – the strange force that can distort reality – fascinated Kukučín. In his short novel *Dies irae* (1893), written before his departure from Prague, he continues to develop his portrayal of the greedy personality. A wealthy peasant, Sýkora, is blinded by his passion for money, though he does not really know what to do with it. When he hides it, he fears for it constantly, so he gives it to the local tavernkeeper, Moses, who plans to increase it through usury. Instead, Moses loses the money. Only the shock of a lost fortune brings Sýkora to his senses. This kind of resolution was typical of Kukučín's Christian view: he tried to restore some balance. Interestingly, his time in Prague did not result in urban tales. The few short sketches from his life there did not result in any serious change of direction; he remained faithful to his commitment to produce literature that would show the village in a new light. Even his first and not very successful attempt at a play, *Komasácia* (Surveying, 1889), is placed in a village.

After completing his medical studies, Kukučín decided to practice medicine on the island of Brač, off the Dalmation coast. He was influenced in this decision by his friendship with a wealthy Croatian family whom he met in Prague. From this period (1894–1907), his most remarkable prose work is the novel *Dom v stráni* (The house on a hill, 1904). This novel represents, in many ways, a radical departure for Kukučín. It had been possible – indeed, it was probably emotionally necessary – for him to keep his ties with the Slovak village intact throughout the years of his stay in Prague. The move to Brač was an entirely different matter: he married Perica Didolič there and settled on the island permanently. At the same time, the focus of his literary interest shifted from the Slovak village to the Dalmatian village. He was now writing in Slovak about a foreign people and sending this material to Slovakia for publication. *Dom v stráni*, written between 1902 and 1904, was published in 1903–04 in *Slovenské pohl'ady*.

The grand themes of this novel are those of all great literature: love and death. The question of the nature of true love is contemplated in the story of the infatuation of Niko Dubčič, a landowner's son, with Katica Berac, a peasant girl of uncommon beauty. Even though their parents have grave doubts about this uneven match, Niko's mother and Katica's father decide to allow them to meet. This wise decision eventually leads Niko to reassess his commitment to Katica and see that what attracted him to her was not real love, but physical attraction. Although Niko has a sincere desire to get closer to the people by overcoming a class difference, which he does not consider a serious impediment in his relationship, it turns out that he has underestimated the quality of this obstacle. His friend Zandome, a businessman, explains:

> I just wanted to show that there are certain differences, barriers that you should not cross, if you don't want to be punished. Life itself erected them, slowly, unobserved, and now there they stand, and nobody knows what their purpose is ... But he who would ignore them, belittle them, or pull them down would be courting revenge. On the other side of the barrier is another atmosphere, another manner, another kind of understanding, moods, and, I could even say, another faith and religion ... What do we have in common with peasants? We live with them, we meet them daily, but still, how many dark, mysterious things there are in their life and their ways. We don't understand them, and stand before them puzzled in our incomprehension.

Niko eventually understands the failure of his relationship with Katica, and with help of such friends as Zandome he can even rationalize it. Things are different for Katica. Her reactions are much more emotional, even sensual. It is not easy for her to give up her dream of escape from peasant drudgery, for this possibility had influenced her decision to leave Pasko, to whom she made her promise, and begin seeing Niko. That her dream was unrealizable is too hard to bear. Only the impending death of her father restores her equanimity and sound judgement. Thus the themes of love and death intertwine, and she decides to return to Pasko, who has faithfully awaited her.

Apart from this two-volume novel, Kukučín wrote a number of short stories and travel stories. When the people on the island where he lived decided to go to South America in search of better living conditions, he decided to join them. After he arrived in Punta Arenas, Chile, he was very busy, but he nonetheless continued with his literary work. An unusual and lengthy travelogue, *Prechádzka po Patagónii* (A promenade in Patagonia, 1922) widened the framework of the genre to admit philosophical and social reflections. A somewhat lighter travelogue, *Dojmy z Francúzska* (Impressions of France, 1923), reflected the author's feelings about his return to his homeland, the humorous passages perhaps anticipating the pleasurable experience of his homecoming.

However, Kukučín was disappointed with conditions in Czechoslovakia. After trying, and failing, to find a suitable place in this new society, he once more moved to his wife's homeland, Yugoslavia, where he spent the rest of his life. His energies as a writer were spent on several major projects: a novel on Croatian exiles in Latin America, *Mat' volá* (Mother is calling, 1927) and a number of historical novels dealing with the national revival. This was the time of a new definition of the Slovak nation, but also one full of misunderstandings, particularly among those who should have been Kukučín's closest and most understanding friends: the Czech revivalists. Thus, in *Lukáš Blahosej Krasoň* (1929), Kukučín writes of the years 1843–44, the time of codification of the Slovak language. It was an awkward time in Czech-Slovak relations, since many Czech patriots considered this Slovak action as an attempt at separation and a diversion from the struggle against the common enemy – the Hapsburg monarchy. However, Slovaks acted out of an inner need, their strong desire to codify a language that did not have a permanent, *written*, literary counterpart. As well, the Slovaks were more concerned with Hungarian than with Austrian oppression.

Dealing with these controversial issues, Kukučín draws fascinating portraits of Czech society, particularly such pseudo-nationalist types as his character Beznožka, an individual prepared to compromise his beliefs for egotistical reasons. Less realistic is his gallery of Slovak characters, such as the idealized Lukáš Blahosej Krasoň. One has the impression that Kukučín used contemporary history to produce an apologia for his lack of success in his own country, which could not find room for one of its most brilliant writers.

Kukučín's next novel, *Bohumil Valizlosť Zábor* (1930), also set in the 1840s, showed the impact of the Štúr movement on the Orava region, and correctly gauged the need to give the movement prominence at a time when many Czechs considered Štúr a separatist rather than a nationalist hero. Present again is the sure touch of a writer who knows village people. His accurate descriptions of the relations between the lower nobility and the common folk express the intricacy of a situation that presented the nobility with the impossible choice between submitting to the Magyars and losing their property as a result of their support of Štúr.

When Kukučín's two historical novels appeared posthumously, the literary situation in Slovakia was much changed. A spirit of experimentation and an atmosphere of irreverence and disillusionment reigned following the cataclysmic world war, along with a genuine search for new truths and a new, stronger faith, which some found in the ideas of nationalism, others in leftism, still others in the eternal teachings of religion. In this milieu, Kukučín's work, particularly that from his last period, has an unusual flavour. It is a timeless literature, seemingly oblivious to the work of those who were preparing the soil for the arrival of the twentieth-century masters of prose, such as J.C. Hronský and M. Urban.

However, a special place of distinction must be reserved for the work of four women writers: Terézia Vansová, Elena Maróthy-Šoltésová, Ľudmila Riznerová-Podjavorinská, and Božena Slančíková-Timrava. Although some of them survived into the 1940s and 1950s, their best efforts were produced, on the whole, before 1918.

SLOVAK WOMEN WRITERS

Terézia Vansová (1857–1942)

Vansová was a pioneering personality who opened the door for other Slovak women writers through her writing and her editorship of the first Slovak journal for women. She was born into a family with many contacts among the outstanding personalities of the national revival, such as Andrej Sládkovič, Ján Francisci, and August Škultéty. Though she did not complete her *gymnasium* education or attend university, she did receive good basic schooling in Zvolenská Slatina, where her father was a Lutheran pastor. She then spent two years improving her German and her Hungarian and reading voraciously. This lack of formal education was a common situation for Slovak women, and other Slovak women writers (Maróthy-Šoltésová, Riznerová-Podjavorinská, and Slančíkova-Timrava) had to educate themselves. In fact, one of the most important campaigns in the journalism of both Vansová and Maróthy-Šoltésová was a call for improved educational opportunities for Slovak women.

Vansová, not surprisingly, married a Lutheran pastor, and they lived in the German village of Lomnička in the Spiš region. Her first literary effort, *Moje piesne* (My songs, 1875) was a selection of sentimental and often awkward verses. This was followed by mature poems (written in German) that express the pain and hopelessness experienced by a mother who has lost her son, a loss Vansová herself had suffered. They were published in the local journal, *Karpathenpost* (1881–82). In 1881, her husband was posted to Píla, where Vansová spent the next thirty years, flourishing as a writer, organizer, and editor.

She edited the first magazine for Slovak women, *Dennica* (Morning star, 1898–1914), which offered a variety of materials reflecting its unique position. Next to stories, poems, and essays by women writers were articles on fashion, recipes, advice on marital life and social etiquette, and information on the women's movement elsewhere in the world.

As a writer, Vansová is remembered chiefly for her prose. Her early pieces were heavily influenced by the German sentimental and romantic prose that she had read in popular German magazines, and she never completely turned her back on the romantic influence. However, she had matured considerably by the end of the 1880s, as evidenced in *"Prvotina"* (First publication, 1889), in which she parodied the kind of writing that she herself was guilty of. Many of her short stories have exotic elements, betraying her impatience with the established subject matter of Slovak prose. Her main interest was the subject of relationships in the world of prejudice. In *"Rozsobášení"* (Divorced, 1884), a marital breakdown is caused equally by misunderstandings between husband and wife and the meddling and prejudice of others. In *"Obete márnomyselnosti"* (Victims of vanity, 1890), Marta's marriage to the vain and foppish Toházy collapses due to Toházy's urbanized moral degeneration. Having learned her lesson, Marta finds happiness with her step-brother, Pavol. Psychologically better motivated is the novella *Chovanica* (Orphan, 1891), despite its sentimental elements.

A decade later, Vansová's *Sirota Podhradských* (The Podhradský orphan, 1889) appeared. This was the first Slovak novel written by a woman. It was a gothic novel, again marked with the influences of German romantic and sentimental fiction. However, these elements are less important than Vansová's characterizations and psychological insight into her characters, the moral dimension of complex relationships, and the dynamic and dramatic construction of the plot. The novel was well received by S.H. Vajanský despite its lack of nationalist propaganda.

Much more realistic in conception is Vansová's interesting travelogue *Pani Georgiadesova na cestách* (The travels of Mrs Georgiades, 1897). Through the eyes of the fictional Mrs Georgiades, the author presents fresh and intelligent observations of Prague at the time of an anthropological exhibition; the state of the nationalist movement; historical and geographical digressions; and, most importantly, the state of Czech-Slovak relations in 1895.

Vansová tried her hand at play-writing, mostly comedies such as the satirical *L'ubezní hostia* (Dear guests, 1901). Her most successful play, however, was a drama, *Svedomie* (Conscience, 1897).

After 1918, Vansová wrote memoirs, edited her older writings, continued her publishing venture, and even produced some novels, such as the historical *Kliatba* (Curse, 1926)and the love story *Sestry* (Sisters, 1930). However, this work was overshadowed by that of those who started writing after 1918, a fate Vansová was to share with the other outstanding pioneers of women's fiction. Nevertheless, her accomplishments, as an original writer, an editor, and an important voice in the intellectual history of Slovakia, are secure.

Elena Maróthy-Šoltésová (1855–1939)

Maróthy-Šoltésová, with her many-faceted activity – literary, critical organizational – is another in the first, pioneering, generation of Slovak women writers. One reason for her enthusiasm may have been her illustrious family background: her father, Daniel Maróthy, was a poet of the Štúr generation who brought his family up in the spirit of Slovak nationalism during this most reactionary period.

Well connected with the realities of the life of the village folk whom her father served as a Protestant minister, Moróthy-Šoltésová was also well educated for her time, attending women's colleges in Lučenec and Spiš. Married at twenty to a wealthy businessman, she moved with him to Turčianský Svätý Martin, the centre of Slovak cultural life, where she spent the rest of her life.

Her literary début was very auspicious: her first work, *"Na dedine"* (In the Village, 1881), won her a prestigious literary prize of fifty francs in gold. In this and subsequent short stories, she used her finely honed powers of observation to create memorable portraits of the village milieu, achieving a great deal of success with the realistic portraiture of her story *"V čiernickej škole"* (The Čiernice school, 1891).

Much more ambitious is her novel *Proti prúdu* (Against the current, 1894). It is the story of a Slovak *zeman*, Savelský, who regains his national identity after meeting a highly inspirational woman, Olga. Savelský marries Olga and, under her influence, soon becomes a spokesman for the Slovak cause, despite the activity of many enemies. The depiction of a number of similar families gives a picture of a veritable renaissance of the Slovak cause, at a time when it was highly desired but little realized – as some critics, including Martin Kukučín, pointed out. Despite this idealization and insufficient differentiation of the characters' personalities, the novel is a valuable document of this period of national oppression and has worn remarkably well.

The most prominent feature of the novel is the heightened role of women. This reflected the presence of some strong, influential women in Slovak national life, as well as the fact that Maróthy-Šoltésová had become president (1894–1927) of the Slovak women's organization Živena, whose eponymous periodical, *Živena*, she edited for years and to which she contributed many keys essays. In her writings, she repeatedly mentioned and praised Božena Slančíková-Timrava's work. A collection of her essays, *Pohľady na literatúru* (Views on literature) was published in 1958.

Maróthy-Šoltésová's tireless work on behalf of Slovak women is even more impressive seen against the background of the great personal tragedy she suffered – the death of her two children (Elenka, d. 1884; Ivan, d. 1912). She overcame her grief by writing an unforgettable memoir of her children, *Moje deti* (My children, 1923–24). She shows no bitterness and disillusionment in this work; on the contrary, it is imbued with a gentle, lyrical, joyous mood that transforms a mother's pain into a luminous work of art. This memoir is considered the high point of her *œuvre.*

Maróthy-Šoltésová was also important for her encouragement of Slovak women in their quest for better education and a broader worldview. She helped to form their literary and a esthetic taste and was a trusted guide and mentor. Though she was in conflict with men who did not quite understand her motives or aims, her position strikes us today as eminently reasonable, objective, and even anti-radical.

Ľudmila Riznerová-Podjavorinská (1872–1951)

As one of ten children, Riznerová-Podjavorinská was unable to get a good education, and, like many of her predecessors, she had to educate herself. She had help from her uncle, Ľudovít Rizner, a bibliographer, who introduced her to poetry and fiction, and she eagerly began to make her name in both. She was also aware of the nationalist implications of literature. In the absence of statehood, it was literature above all that represented the nation, she wrote in an article in 1899. And she was the first important Slovak woman poet.

Her first collection, *Z vesny života* (From life's spring, 1895), was well received by the critics. The poems are organized as the lyrical journal of a young girl whose emotional and intellectual moods are influenced by natural phenomena. The author's lack of experience and her idealism contrast with the cynicism and unconcern of the world. Compared to the hortatory nationalist poetry of the previous generation, Riznerová-Podjavorinská was impressive for the intimate, melodic, yet passionate character of her poetry.

In her early prose, Riznerová-Podjavorinská continued in the direction charted by Martin Kukučín. This is particularly evident in "Ondráš" (1897), in which Kukučín's "Unawakened" (1866) is quite consciously imitated. Her early attempts contained elements of didacticism and moralizing. Important influences in her work came from Russia (Pushkin, Lermontov, Turgenev) and Bohemia (Němcová, Jirásek). She found her own voice in her best work: "*V octroctve* (In slavery, 1905), "*Blud* (Evil 1906), and "*Žena*" (Wife, 1909).

Žena (1909) is a particularly instructive example of how Riznerová-Podjavorinská was able to shed the moralizing tone or her earlier prose and adopt a very effective and economical style relying on indirection. Iva, a good, honest, and very hard-working woman, marries a widower, Štefan, an insecure and lazy man with five children. Iva manages to reform her husband by showing him the difference between her hard work and his procrastinating. He regains his self-respect and becomes a worthy partner for Iva and a good father to his five children. The story presents opportunities to moralize and become sentimental or maudlin, but Riznerová-Podjavorinská avoids them. Her portrait of a good wife is highly effective, believable, and memorable.

Riznerová-Podjavorinská also wrote stories about the urbanized upper class, but these suffer from her lack of the intimate knowledge of this milieu. As a master of psychological insight into the Slovak peasant, her prose centred on the village is more believable.

When, in 1910, Riznerová-Podjavorinská moved into a small town, cutting her contact with the village, her writing suffered. She abandoned prose for poetry and children's literature. As it was for others' 1918 proved to be a median year that was difficult for her to cross. Her ballads and lyrical poetry are a continuation of the honoured tradition started by the Štúr generation, but they represent a divergence, or perhaps even escape, from the mainstream of Slovak literature after 1918.

However, in her children's literature, Riznerová-Podjavorinská was again doing pioneering work, and she is recognized as the undisputed master of this form. She never condescends, but accepts the openness and indeterminacy of the child's world as her own. Her collections of children's poetry – *Kytka veršov pre slovenské dietky* (A bouquet of poems for Slovak children, 1920), *Veršíky pre maličkých* (Verses for the little ones, 1930), *Medový hrniec* (Coper kettle, 1930), and *Klásky* (Ears of grain, 1930) – maintain the proper balance of playfulness, humour, and fantasy communicated in a melodic, rhythmic, natural manner. Not everything she wrote for children had this lighthearted, playful quality; she also wrote prose dealing with problems which were avoided at that time: *Čarovné skielka* (Magical glass, 1931) and *Baránok Boží* (Lamb of God, 1932).

Although Riznerová-Podjavorinská was the first serious woman poet and an important writer of realistic prose, she will be remembered as Slovakia's best children's author.

Božena Slančíková-Timrava (1867–1951)

Like Riznerová-Podjavorinská, Slančíková-Timrava was born into a large family of eleven children. Her father was very supportive and encouraged his offspring to develop their individual talents. He educated them himself, as Lutheran pastors were wont to do at the time, and sent Božena to a private school in Banská Bystrica for a year. The children were expected to read a great deal, and they even published their own magazine, where Slančíková-Timrava's first writings appeared. Her older sister was also a writer, whose work was published in *Slovenské pohľady* (Slovak Views).

Slančíková-Timrava's life was spent in two villages, Polichno and Ábelová. This determined her choice of subject matter. Despite the fact that she wrote some 140 poems between 1886 and 1897, her prose was dominant from the very beginning. In fact, her poetry was largely uninventive and imitative, while her prose was written in opposition to the sentimentality that her predecessors had found so seductive.

The main concern of sentimental prose of the time was romantic love. Slančíková-Timrava set out to write about anti-romantic relationships. The result is a realistic and ironic look at men and women. At the same time, she brought to her stories a certain amount of bias in her underestimation of the role of passion and overestimation of the practical, financial aspects of courtship and marriage. In "*Kandidát ženby*" (Marriage candidate, 1893), a confirmed bachelor is the object of a determined woman's attention. The man, Juro Agač, has no chance to escape; he finally gives in to the skilful Božena's suit, but once he agrees to the marriage, it turns out that Božena's action is motivated by a rather practical concern: she is looking for someone to support her for the rest of her life. She is not in love.

After her apprenticeship with this type of counter-sentimentality, Slančíková-Timrava decided to broaden her range, creating a unique style in Slovak literature: "democratic prose." The main characteristic of this style was that instead of a principal motive surrounded by a number of lesser ones, the reader is presented with several motives of apparently equal importance. Only the conclusion, or epilogue, uncovers which of the competing motives turned out to be of decisive importance. In the novella *Veľké šťastie* (Great happiness, 1906), Slančíková-Timrava presents the clash of two worlds: peasants and their masters. These worlds are further fragmented into the characters' personas and their inner selves. The female characters are depicted as having rich interior lives, which society suppresses, forcing them to wear the mask of hypocrisy. One woman resists this: Jozefa (or Joža) Jakubovicová, seemingly Slančíková-Timrava's own voice. Like Dostoevsky's Myshkin in *The Idiot*, Joža tells everyone the truth, no matter how unpleasant it is. Her determination is the result of a great deal of personal suffering, which seems to justify her behaviour.

Much more controversial and critical is the novel *Skúsenosť* (Experience, 1902). In this work, based on a very unpleasant personal experience, the time when she lived with Hviezdoslav's widow – ostensibly as her companion, but in reality as a servant of sorts – Slančíková-Timrava gives vent to her disappointment with those who are supposed to be the moral leaders of the nation. Instead, she finds phonies whose apparent attachment to national culture and the nationalist cause is a shallow social convention, hiding a greedy desire for assimilation, and the aping of the "greater culture."

In her village prose, Slančíková-Timrava explores the conflict between the emotions and property in marriage. The idea of combining two properties and forming a sizeable estate overshadows the shaky relationship that augurs poorly for a successful union (*"Na jednom dvore"* [In the same courtyard], 1904). Conversely, a good match is undermined by the financial – or, rather, property – "unworthiness" of one of the partners (*"Žiadna radosť"* [No joy], 1911).

Slančíková-Timrava's village prose eventually moved away from her preoccupation with marital finances to touch upon larger issues of the time. The problem of emigration was acute at the turn of the century. There were two reasons for this: intensifying Magyarization, and industrialization, which depressed the value of agriculture and lessened the importance of the village. Slančíková-Timrava explored the complex economic, social, psychological, and family aspects of emigration in

"Tá zem vábna" (That tempting land, 1907), and she also considers the life of emigrants in their new countries.

The backwardness of villages became an acute problem in this period as well. Gone was the time when the village was an ideal habitat for the nationally conscious Slovak who could not feel at home in a city dominated by German or Magyar elements. On the one hand, the proportion of Slovaks in the towns was rising; on the other hand, the quality of life in the villages was deteriorating. The natural conservatism of the village – a positive feature when it meant survival of the Slovak nation – became a handicap in a time of revolutionary changes. The Slovak leaders residing in Turčianský Svätý Martin (the conservative faction dominating the nationalist movement at the time) were still committed to the comfortable fiction of the pastoral village of yesteryear. Slančíková-Timrava pressed this message home in *"Ťapákovci"* (The Ťapák family, 1914).

A family of sixteen, the patriarchal Ťapáks live together in a small house, in a passive, inarticulate kind of existence, uninterested in the world outside their house. They fearfully cling to the heritage of their forebears without concern for the present, ignoring the need to adjust to the changes that are being thrust upon them. Only two women, Anča the Viper and Il'a the Queen, are different. When Il'a the Queen sets out to change the Ťapák clan, she concentrates on her husband, Pal'o. Her effort is successful, but it is contrasted against the tragic character of Anča the Viper, a handicapped old maid. The conflict between Il'a and the clan is a triumph of characterization effectively drawn – through indirection – by other characters, rather than by the narrator.

Like Hviezdoslav's *Krvavé sonety*, Slančíková-Timrava's war fiction is the most authentic depiction, previous to the work of Milo Urban, of the ravages of the war as it played itself out in the Slovak village (*"V čas vojny,"* "War Time," 1917 and *"Hrdinovia,"* "Heroes," 1918).

After 1918, Slančíkova-Timrava continued to write, and her most accomplished work of this period was *"Skon Pal'a Ročku"* (Death of Pal'o Ročka, 1921). This story has been compared to those of Dostoevsky and Urban, because of her deep insight into the character of Pal'o Ročka, whos death reveals the dramatic peripeteia of his life, with its moral fall and renewal, rebellion and acceptance. In a confrontation of two temporal planes, Slančíková-Timrava gives us a dynamic evaluation of human life, in which the past is allowed to mould the present and change the future of the character, whose consciousness is enriched by the realization of impending death.

Slančíkova-Timrava's autobiographical novel *Všetko za národ* (Everything for the nation, 1926) reveals much of her background, from her childhood to the formation of her creative method and its psychological underpinnings. Politically, the work is a statement against the conservative leadership of the Slovak nationalist movement before 1918.

The plays Slančíková-Timrava wrote after 1918 revealed a decline in quality, and their critical reception was rather lukewarm. Her stength is best demonstrated in the short story, of which she proved to be a rare master because of her talent for characterization (often through indirection) and the pervasive irony with which she viewed the society of her time, which endowed her observations with the stamp of objectivity. Her analytical powers enabled her to understand the psychology of her characters to a degree not seen before in Slovak literature. For this reason, she is especially close to such novelists as Urban and Hronský.

REALISM OF THE TRANSITIONAL PERIOD

The last years of the nineteenth century and the beginning of the twentieth saw a quickening of social, national, political, and cultural life in Slovakia. This was due as much to political developments as to the greater availability of education. Young Slovaks were getting an education not only in their homeland, but, often, in Budapest, Vienna, and Prague. In Prague, they founded student societies and grouped themselves in politically and nationally defined bodies such as Detvan and around the periodical *Hlas* (Voice) in Prague, and there were similar organizations in Budapest and Vienna. New political and literary magazines appeared, providing a forum for writers, reviewers, and critics. This was accompanied by a similar burst of activity in Slovak centres in the United States, which would soon exert a powerful influence on the politics of the old country, particularly during the First World War.

Some who wrote during this transitional period, such as Jesenský and Jégé, also managed important contributions after 1918; others, such as Tajovský and Ján Čaják (1863–1944), found themselves at odds with the new literary scene. All of them, however, fulfilled the vital role of a bridge via which the best of the pre-1918 efforts found continuity with liberated Slovak culture. The same can be said of the poetic movement called Moderna, comprising Krasko, Roy, and Gall; the playwright Urbánek; and the critics Vlček, Škultéty, Votruba, and Bujnák.

Josef Gregor-Tajovský (1874–1940)

Tajovský's pseudonym came from the village of Tajov, near Banská Bystrica in central Slovakia, where he was born, the eldest of ten children. He was educated in a Magyar school in Banská Bystrica and then in a teacher's college in Kláštor pod Znievom. After he graduated, in 1893, he returned to his old school in Banská Bystrica, where he taught in Hungarian and Slovak. An ardent nationalist, he was often moved from school to school. A chance meeting with the playwright Ferko Urbánek interested him in the theatre, and when his unwillingness to co-operate with the official policy of Magyarization became a threat to his teaching, he went to Prague, where he enrolled in the Commercial Academy (1898–1900).

Prague was already one of the centres of Slovak student activity. Tajovský joined Detvan and contributed to *Hlas*, a periodical with an ideology resembling Tolstoyan pacifism and politically influenced by T.G. Masaryk. In Detvan, there were lectures on Czech and Russian literature, and Tajovský soon became interested in the work of the Czech historical novelist Jirásek, whom he met, and of Gogol, Tolstoy, Dostoevsky, and Chekhov.

Upon his return to Slovakia, Tajovský began a career in banking, becoming a bank manager in Prešov in 1910. In 1915, he changed careers again, becoming the editor of *Národný hlásnik* (National crier). Drafted in the summer of 1915, he defected to the Russians in December, and became active in the formation of the Czechoslovak Legion in Russia, contributing to its publications.

Tajovský began his literary work with poetry, but Vajanský advised him to abandon poetry in favour of prose and drama. Like many of his predecessors, Tajovský began by going back to folk literature, in the interest of offering readers something authentic. He was careful lest the characterization, speech, or motivation of his characters seemed artificial or stilted. Thus his first two collections of sketches, stories, and tales, *Omrvinky* (Crumbs, 1897) and *Z dediny* (From the village, 1897), often exhibit an almost documentary quality.

One of the utilitarian tenets of Hlasist ideology was the belief, shared by Tajovský, that literature could play a great role in the moral and political regeneration of the Slovak village. This belief coloured his next collection of stories, *Rozprávky* (Fairy-tales, 1900). In *"Do konca"* (To the End), he paints a morally uplifting portrait of his grandfather, who always worried about his family, making sure they would not lack for anything after his death.

In 1904, Tajovský published two more collections. In the second, *Rozprávky pre ľud* (Tales for ordinary people) he dealt with acute problems of the day, such as urbanization, which was transforming some villages into labour pools from which the newly installed industries drew their workers. The social, psychological, and cultural effects of the resulting uprootedness are intimated in the stories. This began a period of social criticism in his work that continued in his next four books of stories, published between 1907 and 1915.

Tajovský's first dramatic work was a successful comedy, *Ženský zákon* (Woman's law, 1900), the subject of which was the sad fact that love and marriage are distorted by considerations of property and finances. This theme has been already introduced by Slovak women writers, but Tajovský's comedy gave it a more effective forum. A happy ending does mitigate the play's seriousness, and in this lies the uniqueness of Tajovský's contribution: he peopled his comedies with wonderfully authentic female characters speaking the believable language of the village. His next play, *Nový život* (New life, 1901), was completely different. He emerged as a sophisticated European dramatist aware of the work of such contemporary giants of theatre as Ibsen and Tolstoy, whose realistic, even naturalistic, direction influenced him. The plot involves the rise and fall of the Jahoda family, who wish to climb the social ladder. The tragic resolution is portrayed as a precondition for the moral regeneration of his characters.

The direction toward a more socially analytical drama is confirmed in *Statky-zmätky* (Estates in confusion, 1909), in which class identification plays a great role in relationships among people. Tajovský's last play before 1918, a psychological examination of adultery, was *Hriech* (Sin, 1911). Eva, the wife of Andrej Kváska, is unfaithful to him during his absence abroad, where he has gone as an emigrant to help his family. Tajovský skilfully draws a complex picture of a woman who analyzes her failure, points to the contributing factors – her husband's absence, the temptations in her environment, and her social position – and suggests the possibility of overcoming the past through renewed commitment to marriage.

After 1918, Tajovský published his memoirs and wrote a number of plays, but these, like Kukučín's later attempts, were out of step with the new literary situation in Slovakia. This similarity with Kukučín is not accidental. Tajovský in many ways continued and further developed Kukučín's work, particularly in his stories. The stress he laid on social aspects, however, was his own.

Janko Jesenský (1874–1945)

Jesenský produced a large body of poetry and prose and is one of the most important twentieth-century Slovak writers. He was the son of a *zeman* active in the nationalist cause who impoverished his family by financially backing his own candidacy for election on behalf of the Slovak National Party. Thus, despite his well-connected and illustrious background, Jesenský was to know poverty and also to learn how a society that had respected his family behaved toward them in a time of adversity.

Despite this reversal of fortune, Jesenský became a lawyer, practising in a number of towns, including Turčiansky Svätý Martin. He started his literary career with poetry. During his stay in Prešov, where he studied law, he wrote over a hundred poems and two comedies (1895). Most of this material, however, can be classed as juvenilia.

Jesenský's first poem, "*Vyznanie*" (Confession), was published in 1897, as was his first short story, "*Pre jeden fúz*" (Because of a Single Hair). It was only in 1905 that his first collection of poems, *Verše* (Verses), reflected his maturity as a writer. This was immediately understood by the critics. In his love poetry, for example, there was a new approach to the emotional turmoil caused by love: a stress on the contradictory nature of a phenomenon heretofore mostly lyricized or romantically portrayed. This new vision of love was accompanied by a novel approach to woman as the protagonist of love poetry, seeing her as an ambivalent "angel and demon." Despite his occasional lapses into cynicism, his displays of emotion were persuasive and authentic.

In 1913, Jesenský published *Malomestské rozprávky* (Small-town tales), a collection of short stories (he was to write some fifty short stories and novellas in all). The target of his gently satirical portraits of small-town characters was the mentality that this environment often produced: an imitative, narrow mind that followed the fashions of the large cities (Budapest, Vienna, Paris) – but, unfortunately, fashions of the most commercial and kitschy variety. He often went further than did Slančíková-Timrava in his dispassionate analyses of the vices of the small-town society.

The war found Jesenský, like Tajovský, unwilling to fight for foreign interests, and he surrendered to the Russians, an experience that he described in *Zo zajatia* (From the prison, 1918). At Tajovský's invitation, he joined the editorial board of *Čechoslovan*, in Kiev, published by the Czechoslovak Legion. Later, he moved to Petrograd, where he wrote *Nástin dejín slovenskej literatúry* (An outline of the history of Slovak literature, 1918), published in Yekaterinburg, which the Czechoslovak Legion occupied shortly after the assassination of the tsar and his family.

After the war, Jesenský became a high-ranking civil servant in the Czechoslovak government, *a župan* (governor of a Slovakian province); after 1928, he became a regional vice-president when the territorial governments were organized into regions. His literary work was put aside for some years, but then he returned with his translations of Russian poetry (mainly Yesenin's), his own poetry, and a two-volume novel, *Demokrati* (Democrats, 1934, 1938), which Šmatlák considers one of the most important works of Slovak prose in the interwar period.

Even more than his sharply written short stories, this novel is the work of a moralist. It is a *Bildungsroman*, concerning the education of young Dr Jan Landík. The fate of the young man fades into the background as the novel becomes a vast social and political panorama of Slovak life. The sceptical, mildly satirical tone of some of his stories is here turned to consistent irony, sarcasm, and biting satire. Because – or in spite – of his high position in the civil service, Jesenský was able to give a very valuable and revealing picture of the politics of his time. He combined the freedom of action of an outsider with the special knowledge of an insider, uncovering the reality behind institutions, customs, and manners.

Jesenský was a defender of the Slovak language in the years when some Czech politicians were suggesting a common Czech language. Later, during the existence of the Slovak Republic (1939–45), he wrote poetry in which he took a stand as a critic of the new republic and its collaboration with Germany. This work was published only after the war.

Ladislav Nádaši-Jégé (1866–1940)

Jégé was born into the family of a very well-educated lawyer with wide cultural interests and a magnificent library. He studied medicine in Prague, where he became the president of Detvan. After publishing a series of satirical stories between 1889 and 1891, he removed himself from the literary world for three decades, busying himself with his medical practice in Dolný Kubín, the town where he spent most of his life.

Perhaps as a result of his medical studies and his reading of Zola, a considerable influence, Jégé brought a new note of naturalism and biological positivism into Slovak literature. However, as was later the case with Slovak surrealism, these styles were of a different variety than their French predecessors, for they were mixed with Christian spirituality. Jégé's characters were motivated to a large degree by biological instincts, and sexuality played a greater role in his work than heretofore seen in Slovak prose.

Jégé is remembered today mostly for his historical novels, *Adam Šangala* (1923) and *Svätopluk* (1928). In *Adam Šangala,* he sets out to deal with the seventeenth-century religious wars that created the deep sectarian division between Catholics and Protestants in Slovakia. He had an original view of history: his characters must deal with their problems in the "here and now," influenced less by historical considerations – great historical events are present in the background of this novel – than by the "natural" conditions of life. The plot is strictly chronological and Jégé stresses the complex interrelationships between characters like the Catholic Adam Šangala and his Lutheran friend Konopka, and contrasts such as that between reasonable Klára and passionate Brigita. Most of the novel, in fact, is dominated not by Šangala, the title character, but by Konopka, who is used by Jégé to introduce the wider historical context.

Svätopluk is an attempt to overcome the schematic, idealistic, and idyllic image of the ancient Slovak ruler that Jégé found in the historical poetry and prose of the revivalist (Štúr) period. His Svätopluk is well-rounded and contradictory, producing a truly revisionist picture. Jégé does not hesitate to tamper with the historical record, which is clearly secondary to his artistic intention. Thus, contrary to the record, Svätopluk is made the head of an embassy sent to Byzantium for the famous invitation that resulted in the mission of saints Cyril and Methodius to Great Moravia. His meeting with the highly developed Byzantine civilization motivates him to modernize his kingdom. To do this, he must do battle with his own primitive instincts and unbridled barbarian sexuality. His activity sets motion a chain of cause and effect that leads inexorably to his murder.

Jégé's next work was a contemporary novel, *Cesta životom* (Journey through life, 1930). Ján Števček, one of the outstanding Slovak critics, saw this novel as an example of "picaresque naturalism," while Krčméry found it altogether too gloomy, but it is an important contribution because of the number of themes it touches upon and Jégé's pioneering method of incarnating a number of key ideas in different characters. The narrator, Jozef Svoreň, is an opportunistic anti-hero, an uprooted Slovak whose loyalty to the Magyars or Slovaks depends on the benefit he can get out of declaring himself for one or the other. The author makes it clear, however, that conditions were such that Svoreň is not only a villain, but also a victim of circumstances. But Svoreň is not excused; the character of Dr Buroš, Svoreň's antipode, provides the reader with a firm norm. Because of this character I see the novel as a fine example of satire, contrasting Svoreň's conditional, "situational" morality against Buroš's more traditional, less pragmatic morality, which easily pierces the hypocrisy.

Jégé's other novels are less appreciated by contemporary critics such as Stanislav Šmatlák, but his *S duchom času* (In the spirit of the times, 1937) is an interesting work, containing a powerful defence of individualism against a potentially evil mass power, though the protagonist, the rich landowner and philanthropist Irena Poradovská, seems too eccentric to be entirely believable. Certainly, she was found unacceptable by the Marxist critics, but this evaluation may be revised in the future. Jégé's theme is the preservation of values despite the pressure and threat of the masses – not the hungry and huddled masses, but the lockstep masses marching to stamp out all individuality. Considering the times, this novel was a timely and courageous cry for personal freedom and human rights.

Jégé's view of human nature was indeed perhaps too gloomy, due to the naturalistic influence that he accepted only too eagerly. Nevertheless, he supplied Slovak literature with a new register of creative methods, characterizations, and philosophical views that were useful to the next generation of writers, who, thanks to him, wrote for a more sophisticated audience.

DRAMA AND CRITICISM

While it was the rare writer who did not try his hand at playwriting, this genre suffered the additional handicap of being dependent on the existence of theatres. Theatrical troupes, the necessary stage professionals, and critics were also in short supply in the second half of the nineteenth century. Nevertheless, by 1900 these obstacles were overcome when a number of theatre clubs appeared following the pioneering activity of the Martin organization Spevokol (Choir). Apart from occasional efforts by prose writers such as Jozef Gregor Tajovský and Terézia Vansová, there were those who were primarily playwrights, such as Pavel Socháň (1862–1941), Jozef Hollý (1879–912), and Vladimír Konštantín Hurban (1884–1950).

The best known and most prolific playwright of the period was Ferko Urbánek (1859–1934), who wrote some sixty plays in sixty years. Unlike writers before him, Urbánek led a peripatetic life, holding jobs as varied as farmer, assistant pharmacist, notary public, farmer again, then postmaster, ending finally as a secretary of the Slovak League in Bratislava. His life was also marked by crippling heart disease, financial disasters, and his wife's death, but these existential problems did not slow the pace of his creativity. He shared his generation's inability to advance artistically beyond the significant milepost of 1918. Although he continued to write, he produced the same kind of plays about the same kind of village and small town, despite the fact that both had been transformed.

His first play was *Snehulienka* (Snow White, 1875). Here, as elsewhere in his *œuvre*, Urbánek uses the established canon of folk-tales and characters in an innovative recasting of traditional plots and themes. Most of his plays were written for small-town audiences and therefore depicted the vicissitudes of the emerging Slovak small-town educated class. *Pokuta za hriech* (Payment for a sin, 1890) and *Diabol v raji manželskom* (The devil and marital bliss, 1899) are skilfully written drawing-room comedies. Although they aimed at entertainment and little more, in the context of Magyarization, comedy was a valuable framework for promoting and legitimizing the public use of the Slovak language.

Urbánek's village plays, like the comedies *Bludár* (Liar, 1900) and *Škriatok* (Dwarf, 1902), were very popular. The difference between his depiction of small-town society and that of village life resides mainly in his somewhat more realistic treatment of the latter. While his drawing-room comedies seemed to avoid the social problems of the day, his village – despite its idealization – was believable because of his occasional castigation of vices such as superstition (*Škriatok*) and alcoholism (*Pytliakova žena* [Poacher's wife], 1934).

Contemporary critics were not very complimentary to Urbánek, despite the fact that his plays were treasures of folk humour, proverbs, and customs and were frequently performed by Slovak theatres at home and abroad. The reason for this disdain was that Urbánek was ideologically conservative and a Catholic activist, serving at one time as secretary of the St Adalbert Society, a leading Catholic institution and publishing house. Consequently, he advocated a return to the virtuous life and the avoidance of sin, rather than political involvement and ideological commitment. Nor should the main feature of his plays remain unmentioned: a comforting picture of Slovak village and small-town life *before* the malaise of uprootedness infected it. If we can understand the need for such a comforting picture in the personal life of the author, we might also see its merit in view of the discomforting times that all of Slovak society experienced during and after the First World War.

In the heyday of the Štúr generation, the most prominent *Štúrovci* were also writing literary criticism. This was true of succeeding generations of writers as well, notably Vajanský and Kukučín. Before the end of the nineteenth century, many professional critics and literary scholars were employed in wider organizational activities, including editing, publication, and general advancement of the nationalist cause.

Jozef Škultéty (1853–1948) lived through enormous historical changes and provided a living link between the survivors at the Štúr movement, the period of the founding of Matica slovenská (1863), its suppression (1875), its reopening (1919), the founding of the Czechoslovak Republic (1918), its collapse (1939), its re-emergence (1945), and the Communist take-over (1948). Educated as a teacher, Škultéty made a career in Budapest as the editor of a teacher's journal and the author of textbooks for Slovak schools. He refused an offer to work for the Hungarian ministry of education and instead moved to Turčianský Svätý Martin, where he worked as a bank clerk and as editor of *Národnie Noviny*, for which he had been the Budapest correspondent. He stayed there for forty years, taking over the editorship of the paper from Vajanský. More important for Slovak literature was his work in the leading Slovak literary jurnal, *Slovenské pohľady*, which he edited first with Vajanský, then alone from 1890, managing to attract outstanding Slovak writers. After a visit to Russia, he tried to introduce into Slovakia the major Russian writers in translation (he himself translated works by Gogol, Tolstoy, and Turgenev). He wrote, in Hungarian, *A History of Slovak Literature* (1911) for an encyclopaedic publication about international literature published in Budapest. After 1918, he was named – along with Jaroslav Vlček – director for life of Matica slovenská and became a professor as Comenius University in Bratislava. He edited the works of Sládkovič, Hviezdoslav, Kukučín, Hollý, and others. His *magnum opus* is the voluminous *Stodvadsaťpäť rokov zo slovenského života* (One hundred and fifty years of Slovak Life, 1920), in which he defended the Slovak cause against the bugbear of "Czechoslovakism."

Jaroslav Vlček (1860–1930), the son of a Czech father and a Slovak mother, studied in Banská Bystrica and Prague, graduating from Charles University with a degree in Czech and German. By education and by circumstance, he seemed ideally placed to be an interpreter of Slovak literature in Prague and of Czech literature in Slovakia. Indeed, this became his mission. In 1881, he published *Literatúra na Slovensku, její vznik, rozvoj, význam a úspěchy* (Literature in Slovakia: Its origin, development, significance, and achievement), which served as the first draft for his classic of literary historiobiography, *Dejiny literatúry slovenskej* (History of Slovak literature, 1890). This work, despite some omissions and shortcomings, such as his lack of appreciation for the Bernolák movement and for Catholic authors, is a valuable tool for literary historiographers seeking informed and scholarly criticism prior to 1918. Vlček established the reputations of Hviezdoslav and Kukučín as leading Slovak writers. He published a monograph on Pavel Josef Šafárik (1896), became a professor at Charles University in Prague (1898), and wrote several works on Czech literature. He was also among the organizers of Detvan (1882). Most significantly, he was placed at the helm of Matica slovenská in 1919, together with Škultéty, and was responsible for editions of Kollár, Hurban, Štúr, and other major Slovak writers.

Other critics worthy of mention are František Votruba (1880–1953) and Pavel Bujnák (1882–1933). After an apprenticeship as the editor of several Slovak dailies and weeklies, Votruba took over the editorship of *Dennica* from Terézia Vansová and turned this literary magazine into a tribune of the best Slovak literature. In 1909, his essay *Z novšej literatúry* (From recent literature) championed the cause of Jesenský and Moderna and defended Ivan Krasko's poetry. Also important was his work as the editor of *Prúdy* (Currents, 1909–14), a literary magazine for Slovak youth. In his literary criticism, he paid as much attention to new authors (*Tajovský*, 1924; *Ivan Krasko*, 1926) as to older ones such as Palárik, Kráľ, and Vajanský. After the Second World War, he published *Kniha slovenského homoru* (A book of Slovak humour, 1949).

Bujnák studied Protestant theology in Bratislava, and philosophy and Oriental philology in Leipzig. Posted to Budapest as a pastor, he attended courses in Hungarian literature and classical languages there. His *"O najnovšej našej poetickej literatúre"* (On our most recent poetry, 1907) and *"Realizmus a mladá slovenská spisba* (Realism and the young writers of Slovakia, 1912–13, in *Prúdy*) provided a refreshing approach to the latest Slovak literature from a critic well versed in international literature. Like Votruba, he appreciated Hviezdoslav (*Pavel Országh-Hviezdoslav*, 1919), but, unlike Votruba, he did not have a high regard for Krasko or Slančíková-Timrava. He wrote *Stručné dejiny čs. literatúry po Štúra* (Concise history of Czechoslovak literature till Štúr, 1923); a more substantial contribution was *Slovenská poetika* (Slovak poetics, 1921), co-authored with Ján Menšík.

MODERNA

This poetic movement of the beginning of the twentieth century can be seen as a local variety of symbolism, which, in its Slovak application, is a reaction to tendencies and influences from a variety of sources, domestic and foreign. Certainly, Hviezdoslav's work must be mentioned in connection with Slovak symbolist poetry, but the new generation was unusually well read and informed, as the work of Krasko, Roy, and Gall suggests, and so the Czech symbolists (Brezina, Karásek) were read side by side with the French (Verlaine). All in all, some one dozen poets can be associated with this movement, led by its most characteristic representative, Ivan Krasko.

Ivan Krasko (1876–1958)

Krasko, a descendant of the Ján Botto, was himself named Ján Botto. His pseudonym was a practical means to prevent the confusing of the two; it was suggested by S.H. Vajanský. Educated in Hungarian, German, and Romanian secondary schools, Krasko then studied chemistry in Prague. Like other Slovak students before him, he took part in Detvan, acting as an officer from 1900 to 1903. After his studies, he worked for years as a chemical engineer in the desolate, depressing region near Klobúky and Slané, an area that inspired some of his poetry. The war took him to Poland, Russia, and Italy; after it ended, he continued his studies in Bratislava and Prague, earning his doctorate. In 1923, he was elected a member of the Academy of Sciences.

In Krasko's beginnings we can chart the gradual process by which he defined his unique voice through confrontation with Hviezdoslav, the Romanian poet Mihail Eminescu (whom he translated), and finally Paul Verlaine. Verlaine's poem *Art poétique* influenced his *Poetika starej lyriky* (Poetics of Old Lyrical Poetry) and became a programmatic statement of the acceptance of symbolism.

Krasko wrote two collections of poetry: *Nox et solitudo* (Night and loneliness, 1909) and *Verše* (Verses, 1912). His work reveals a sensitive and melancholy soul (the poem "Solitude"), meditating on the mysteries of existence and the place of love in an indifferent world. Often, he uses the form of an interior monologue, an analytical and philosophical examination that is as much a personal catharsis as it is a castigation of the vices of the world. He ranges from a deeply personal examination of conscience to cursing the evils of the world. Thus, in "It is Getting Dark," he writes:

Oblaky nízko sú, tak letia, letia ...!
Žaluje zúfale žaloby marné
ktos príliš úbohý z šíreho sveta,
že veril, že čakal, že stárne, stárne ...

The clouds, keep flying so low, so low ...!
A poor wretch from afar
vainly hurls his desperate complaints
that he believed, and waited, and is geting old, so old ...

Typically, the dominant symbols of light and darkness are alchemized into contrasting pairs of hope and resignation, belief and scepticism, human fellowship and loneliness. These do not inhabit exclusively the poet's personal domain, but reach out into the social domain. Krasko is a poet of both the private and the public spheres.

Verše dedicated to his future wife, comprises twenty-seven poems ranging from subjective lyrics to poems with a nationalist emphasis. Some wistfully hark back to loves gone by, as in "*Dnes zore*" ("Today's Daybreak"):

And we wanted to catch each other's eye openly,
but they were too narrow, too cold to see …
What kind of sadness is it if it hurts more
when the moon is scarlet and cheerless,
in the shiny frost?

Then, as a contrast to the personal lyrics, comes the rebellious spirit calling for action in the widely anthologized poem *"Otrok"* ("Slave"):

I am the one who ripened under the slave-driver's whip,
under a whip that reopens the unhealed wounds,
so that none of them will ever, ever heal again.
My bent back is afraid to straighten itself,
but in my lowered look there still burns hidden fire …

However, the social protest does not sound alien here, because of the dramatic tension built into each poem. For all the analytical depth with which he endowed his work, Krasko also brought to Slovak poetry a particular melodiousness of his own, through his tendency to relax the rhythmic component of his verse – a tendency that was to strengthen in the modern period, after 1918.

Vladimír Roy (1885–1936)

Educated in Bratislava, with theological studies in Scotland, Roy was a Lutheran pastor who made his name as a poet and a leading translator from English (Shakespeare, Dickens, Galsworthy, Wells), German (Goethe, Hauptmann), and French (Dumas, Baudelaire).

Roy's poetic work attempts to bridge Hviezdoslav and Krasko. As with Krasko, a dichotomy is present, expressed in contrasting pairs such as faith versus science; progress versus death; the eternal versus change. His Christian world-view did help him to achieve balance and order in disorienting times. The poems he wrote between 1908 and 1920 were collected in *Keď miznú hmly* (When the mists depart, 1920) and *Rosou a tŕním* (Through the dew and thorns, 1921). In the first collection, he attempts to incorporate the best he found in the Slovak tradition, particularly Hviezdoslav, into the new poetics typified by the symbolism of Moderna. Besides being a symbolist, Roy was also an impressionist, which becomes apparent in his second collection. The poems published later and collected in 1927 show his tendency to find philosophical explanations for his problems and, not surprisingly, to explain them with the help of Christian mysticism, a tendency already observable in his second collection.

Among the Moderna poets, Ivan Gall (1885–1955) deserves mention. Although he published fewer than fifty poems (collected in *Odkaz,* [Message], 1956), they were written with the desire to enliven what he saw as the "monotonous manner of writing poetry," as he wrote to Vansová in 1906. His work sounded a new, melodious note in the repertoire of Slovak poetry.

7 Modern Literature (1918–1990)

The First World War ushered in the modern age, and, more relevantly to Slovaks, it broke up the Austro-Hungarian Empire. The creation of a new state – Czecho-Slovakia – from its ruins stopped the Hungarian nationalist pressure that by the end of nineteenth century had led to large-scale emigration of Slovaks to North and South America. It also opened the way for reinforcing the social and cultural accomplishments of the national revival. Finally, it enabled the Slovaks to produce an educated and ambitious new generation that could put to rest the very real fears of those who had seen the nation disappearing through assimilation and emigration before the war.

However, the historical mileposts are only imperfectly reflected in the literature. The assimilation of new realities is never immediate: the most representative writers of the postwar period, Hronský and Urban, were still writing about prewar Slovakia a decade later. Similarly, the breakup of Czechoslovakia due to the Munich betrayal of 1938 and the subsequent establishment of the Slovak Republic (1939–45) were such a shock that no contemporaneous major literary work attempted to come to terms with it. Less than three years after the war came the Communist take-over, and with it harsh administrative controls over culture, curtailing the freedom of expression that writers had managed to preserve during the war years. It was only after 1956 that there was a partial thaw, followed by a further administrative retreat in the 1960s. Then, the Soviet invasion of August, 1968, froze the liberalizing tendencies of the Dubček regime. Nevertheless, by the mid-1970s, it again became possible for Slovak writers to publish works of quality. Administrative control collapsed in November, 1989, during the "Velvet Revolution" that ushered in a non-communist government. This arrangement proved only temporary; in 1993, the federation broke up and the Slovak Republic was formed. Similar revolutions took place across central Europe as a result of changes that had started in Poland and accelerated after Mikhail Gorbachev came to power. Gorbachev was the first postwar Soviet leader who was reconciled to an independent central Europe (or was simply too busy saving the USSR from imminent collapse to worry much about preserving the Soviet empire).

It was only after 1918 that Slovak literature could fully mature and create a complete literary universe of its own. The very real existential problems caused by the attempted liquidation of Slovak culture through Magyarization disappeared. Complete artistic freedom made its appearance in 1918, when Slovakia was granted "cultural autonomy." The positive aspect of this momentous change for liberated Slovak culture was somewhat tempered by a paternalistic attitude emanating from Prague. It should not be assumed that this paternalism was always ill-meant and unjustified; from Prague also came tremendous support and help, particularly in the cultural and educational fields. Matica slovenská was re-established in 1919; Comenius University was opened the same year, staffed mostly by Czech professors; the Slovak National Theatre opened in 1920, again with much Czech help. Gradually, the foundation was established – if not from scratch, then, at any rate, from modest beginnings – to build the wide spectrum of cultural and social institutions necessary for a healthy cultural life. Much of what was accomplished, however, was later dissipated by unwise political and cultural policies, which, at their worst, promoted an anachronistic ideal of one state, one nation, and one culture unacceptable to Slovaks.

In all fairness, a fateful ambiguity crept into the very first political statement published by independent Slovak politicians, the Slovak National Council, on October 30, 1918, known as the Declaration of the Slovak Nation. It was promulgated at a meeting in Turčianský Svätý Martin, where Slovakia was declared a nation and at the same time "a Slovak branch of the unified Czechoslovak nation." Thus, two nations were stipulated: one Slovak and one Czechoslovak. This led to misunderstandings, confused government policies, enmity, and even tragedy. Curiously, Slovak literature did not seem to suffer, so strong were the foundations built by Štúr and his followers. But politically, it led to all sorts of excesses, including Czech chauvinism and Slovak Czechophobia. For example, the backlash that led to the super-nationalism of some writers during the existence of the Slovak Republic (1939–45) can be ascribed not to some inbred propensity for political extremism, but to a desperate desire for national self-assertion. This need has now been satisfied by democratization of the political process, which has given the Slovaks political independence.

Examining these seventy years historically, we can distinguish three periods, which coincide with the three main accomplishments of Slovak literature during this time. All three were launched by revolutionary changes.

The period from 1918 to 1938 was one of building the new state that had been ushered in by the collapse of the Austro-Hungarian Empire. The continuing dominance of poetry gradually gave way to prose, culminating in the novels of Milo Urban and Josef Cíger Hronský. The roots of the Slovak surrealist movement are found in this period (Rudolf Fábry published his collection of poems *Ut'até ruky* [Severed hands] in 1935). The same can be said of lyrical prose, since its main practitioner, Hronský, matured as a writer in the 1930s (his *Jozef Mak* was published in 1933). The main significance of this period was the development of a complete scale of literary expression, and the broadening and deepening of Slovak literature.

From 1938 to 1948 was a period that saw the dismemberment of Czechoslovakia, the creation of the Slovak Republic (1939–45), and the re-establishment of Czechoslovakia (1945). In this decade, two literary movements dominated: lyrical prose Hronský, L'udo Ondrejov, Margita Figuli) and the Slovak surrealist movement, which mobilized an impressive group of leading poets, artists, and critics. Finally, Ján Smrek and E.B. Lukáč, as well as Catholic poets such as Valentín Beniak, P.G. Hlbina, and Janko Silan, rounded out the poetic counterpart of this period, which contained such important works as Hronský's *Pisár Gráč* (Gráč the clerk, 1940) and Tatarka's *Panna zázračnica* (Wondrous virgin, 1944). Thus, the politically controversial period left two strong literary movements to posterity, along with a number of talented authors. In the present time of building the new Slovak Republic, the importance of this period will no doubt grow.

The years between 1948 and 1989 comprised contradictory and controversial period. Stifling administrative control over culture (particularly during the first decade) resulted in years of stagnation and socialist realist poetry and novels. This was followed by a partial thaw, with the first liberalizing tendencies becoming visible in 1956 in Tatarka'a *Démon súhlasu* (Demon of conformism, 1956) and A. Bednár's *Hodiny a minuty* (Hours and minutes, 1956). A decade of experimentation in the 1960s was followed by the mature novels that appeared in the 1970s and 1980s (by Šikula, Ballek, Habaj, Jaroš, and others). This period ended with the astonishing collapse of the communist regime and the installation of a largely non-communist government led by the dissident playwright Václav Havel.

The three periods are of unequal lengths, but chronological time is a poor guide to their relative significance. Judged on their accomplishments – lyrical prose, surrealism, and the contemporary novel, respectively – they seem relatively equal, for the first period prepared the ground for the eventual flourishing of surrealism and the contemporary novel.

The First World War was a powerful presence in the literature that followed the establishment of the new republic in 1918, particularly in the novels of Hronský and Urban. This was not unique to Slovak writers. Everywhere in Europe, books were published reflecting the general atmosphere of disillusionment and nihilism that followed the horror of the war. The mood of scepticism and moral relativism was not adopted wholesale by Slovak writers, though it found some minor practitioners. Its main significance was that it acted as the midwife of modernity wherever traditional support for religion collapsed. Slovakia, a nation with a strong and still vigorous Catholic tradition and an equally determined Lutheran minority, was on the whole immune to the excesses of modernity that announced themselves after 1918 in a variety of isms.

Slovakia was not – indeed, could not – be immune to the revolutionary changes that saw the kingdom of Hungary destroyed, and that required everyone, not least writers, to see and interpret the world in a new way. In qualifying "newness," one should be wary, however, of the terms "literary development" and "literary evolution" – expressions very dear to Slovak critics – as explanations for post-1918 Slovak literature. Such Darwinian-Marxian concepts have little utility.

This is particularly true of Slovak literature, which has undergone sudden and unexpected eruptions such as the Štúr movement and surrealism. In trying to cope with such literary phenomena, the interpreters employed the formal concept of development, with its beginning, flourishing, and aftermath. This was understandable, but it is a hindrance in trying to understand Slovak literature after 1918. The quality that appeared after 1918 can be better explained by the new historical situation. Thus, the writing of a Hviezdoslav or a Kukučín, fully formed and mature before 1918, differed from that of a Hronský or an Urban, who came to maturity after 1918.

Slovakia itself may have not changed greatly, but the way it was perceived by the new generation did change. Slovakia advanced from provincial backwater to a position of relative prominence as part of a new and important central European country. Hronský and Urban did not have to agonize over the fact that they wrote in a language that was under attack from a hostile government, as Hviezdoslav and Kukučín had had to. However, they had to come to terms with their situation in a manner that would satisfy the new Slovak, and international, literary context.

The radical nature of the change brought about by the event of 1918 can be seen in the remarkable fact that a number of established authors – apart from Kukučín and Hviezdoslav – such as Ladislav Nádaši-Jégé and Jozef Gregor Tajovský, largely did not reflect in their work the new postwar world and the establishment of the republic, but looked back to the world of their youth. More significantly, their styles remained basically unchanged. Thus their poetics sharply contrasted with the poetics of the new generation – not only with the likes of Hronský and Urban, but also with those who introduced new, modern themes into Slovak literature: Ján Hrušovský (1892–1975), Ivan Horváth (1904–60), Gejza Vámoš (1901–56), and Tido J. Gašpar (1893–1972).

The accomplishments of Urban and Hronský contrast with both older and younger authors. Their work derives from the perennial Slovak village prose eschewed by the likes of Vámoš, Horváth, and Gašpar, but it is formally a highly anti-traditional prose with, in Urban's case, modern expressionistic tendencies, while Hronský introduced and established a strong school of lyrical prose. This peaked during the war years; Ondrejov's *Jerguš Lapin* (1939), Figuli's *Tri gaštanové kone* (Three Chestnut-coloured horses, 1942) František Švantner's *Málka* (1942), and Dobroslav Chrobák's *Drak sa vracia* (Dragon returns, 1943) are examples of the varied, imaginative, and original exploitation of the creative discoveries of Urban and Hronský.

Milo Urban (1904–82)

When Urban published his major work, *Živý bič* (The living whip, 1927), some representatives of the established generation (such as Nádaši-Jégé, but also the younger critic Štefan Krčméry) attacked his depiction of the Slovak village. It seemed to them that he was tampering with reality. In fact, he was experimenting with a new perception, establishing a kind of fictional reality in the general atmosphere of experimentation that involved all European literature after the war, a process whose beginnings went back to the prewar period. Even in his first successful effort, Urban was aware of the larger European literary context.

Urban saw the Slovak village involved in a dynamic process of change. He was the first one to point out the resulting atomization of village culture. Modernity had made encroachments on the village world earlier, but Urban took as his point of departure the convulsions produced by the war. The world before the war entered the village was markedly different from the world in which the war made itself at home. The allegorical arrival of war in the village is one of the great moments in *Živý bič*. In this novel, an expressionist transformation takes place. The fairy-tale world of the village, where myth and legend reside, is gradually displaced by a world of harsh and deadly truths, a delirious, corrupt, and destructive world normally associated with the city. Urban achieved this transformation through the use of striking imagery.

A comparison with Hronský's village reveals a cardinal difference in the two authors' approaches to the same theme. The difference did not lie so much in the diagnosis or analysis of village life; rather, it was in their respective estimates of the hidden forces that could overcome the existing evil they both detected. Hronský's lyricism suggested that an inner, spiritual strength would be needed. While there was a social aspect to the individual failings (the sum total of individual failures being a collective failure), Urban disagreed with Hronský's emphasis on the *spiritual* roots of the problem; for him, religion was an ambiguous force. In *Živý bič*, he opposes the pseudo-religious priest, Letay, to the genuine priest, Mrva, whose mysticism Urban did not denigrate. On the contrary, it fitted his artistic plan; the world was a "bleeding wound," which, according to Adam Hlavaj, the hero of the novel, was acceptable, providing that tragedy led to freedom.

Urban's next attempt to tackle a wider theme was in *Hmly na úsvite* (Daybreak mists, 1930), a portrait of a small factory town with a quickly growing business community. This work suffered from a lack of the unity and intensity that had made his first novel so remarkable. However, he compensated with his psychological insight into a variety of characters and his avoidance of easy solutions such as the adoption of some totalitarian creed. Instead, Urban's hero, in his suffering, finds solace in Christ during a mystical vision.

In the third novel of the trilogy, *V osídlach* (In the trap, 1940), the larger social problems so skilfully recognized and analyzed in the previous works give way to depiction of a smaller number of characters in Bratislava. Still, it is not a portrait of the city or its society, in the sense that he captured the village of Ráztoky in *Živý bič*, but a story of individuals rebelling against their personal destinies.

Urban's works written after the war were of markedly lower quality, with the exception of the charming memoir *Zelená krv: Spomienky hájnikovho syna* (Green blood: remembrances of a gamekeeper's son, 1970). Perhaps it would be fair to say that the farther Urban strayed from his familiar Slovak village, the less sure he was.

Compromise with the world beyond the traditional confines of one's environment, prompted by the blandishments of freedom, is one of the great themes of modern Slovak literature, complementing that of the moral and spiritual uprootedness of the village and the rise of the urbanized individual we presented by Hronský. Since his rehabilitation, in the 1960s, the reputation of Hronský, who died in exile in Argentina, has been steadily growing.

Josef Cíger Hronský (1896–1960)

The old village was Hronský's main preoccupation in the first period of his work, particularly in *Jozef Mak* (1933). The passive, mute protagonist, Jozef Mak, allows the narrator to meditate on the significance of the peasant masses and, by extension, on the human condition. Hronský invested the Slovak village with a magical presence and a lyricism that was to make him the main practitioner of the school of lyrical prose. He had a particularly subtle and sophisticated insight into village life, believing that the Slovak village had a mysterious – if not mystical – depth. Thus, the mute Slovak nation is symbolized by the inarticulate Jozef Mak, who seems to be a man like a million others. Yet, as we are taken into his modest domain, we begin to appreciate the complexities of even a simple peasant life. One concerns his relationship with his wife, whom he betrays with another woman; another is his relationship with the rest of the world. The first relationship is resolved through Mak's gradual realization of his wife's great, selfless love, which he appreciates when it is too late. The other relationship – Mak and the rest of the world – is connected to the religious worldview of the narrator, who stipulates a world ordered by the Divine Providence in which even an insignificant peasant has as important a place as any other person.

Pisár Gráč (Gráč the clerk, 1940), a Dostoevskian novel in the form of a confessional monologue, was an important departure in more than one sense. It was perhaps the first fully mature Slovak urban novel, and thus was particularly influential in the 1960s, when this genre became permanently established in Slovak literature. In this courageous literary experiment, Hronský gradually illuminates the main female character through a series of introspective analyses of other characters and through an imaginary conversation with a dead man. This grotesque device allows the narrator to maintain emotional balance for the tragic, bittersweet ending of the novel, which resolves in an unexpected manner the angry narrator's problem of loneliness.

Hronský's last work of lyrical prose, *Andreas Búr, Majster* (Andreas Bur, the master, 1948), written and published abroad, was called "the completion and the crowning effort of the school of lyrical prose" by one of Slovakia's finest critics, Ján Števček. In Hronský's poetics, lyrical prose destroyed realistic convention by substituting for the objective narrative one that originated in a consciousness that was lyrical and poetic, and thus clashed with the background, which was traditionally realistic. Alternately, Hronský submerged or enveloped realistic action in a lyrical, poetic, even mystical light, which itself served as a background. At times, this consciousness seemed childlike in its fresh impressionism, recalling the well-known device of defamiliarization; yet, in Hronský, the change in focus was not in itself the point. Rather, such a vision was a part of his world-view: it was always integral, never extraneous or exotic. The lyrical figures and symbols existed side by side with the realistic characters, often playing a key role, or "explaining" the characters by suggesting their *raison d'être.* It was this movement that inspired the resurgence of Slovak literature in the 1960s, after the "socialist realist" experiment collapsed – for example, in the work of the key author of a decade of experimentation, Vincent Šikula (b. 1936). Hronský is not only the leading representative of the lyrical-prose movement in Slovak literature, but also the most important prose writer, because he managed to produce at least five major novels. Švantner, Figuli, and Ondrejov all produced one or two remarkable works, but failed to reach the same prominence as Hronský. Finally, Hronský deserves a special place of honour as a skilful manager of the almost defunct Matica slovenská, which he took over in 1932 and turned into a profitable institution. After he emigrated, in 1945 (to Austria, Italy, and Argentina, 1948–60), he remained active in exile as a writer and as the organizer of Matica slovenská Abroad.

Ján Smrek (1898–1982)

Following an eventful childhood, Smrek was drafted to fight in the First World War, which took him as far as Istanbul, Damascus, and Palestine. After studying Protestant theology for several years, he was lured to journalism and editorial work. This led him to Prague, where he published a literary monthly, *Elán* (1930–39 in Prague, 1939–44 and 1946–47 in Bratislava). As an editor, he encouraged the younger generation of writers, improved the level of journalism with his highly cultivated language, and supported Slovak literature by criticizing the Czechoslovakizing tendency.

Smrek was a poet of love and harmony, as well as a tireless organizer. Although he started with brooding, reflective poetry based on symbolist models in *Odsúdený k večitej žízni* (Sentenced to eternal thirst, 1922) he quickly turned to poetry celebrating life, love, and *élan vitale,* influenced by the ideas of Henri Bergson, in *Cválajúce dni* (Galloping days, 1925). As a poet of love, he published the collection *Básnik a žena* (Poet and woman, 1934), in which he tried to capture the evanescent subject of love through a variety of approaches. Identifying with the lyrical hero, he employs a neo-romantic lyrical reflexion in combination with emotional, sentimental, and even prosaic moods. At his best, he arrives at the identification of pure love with pure lyricism.

During the war, Smrek reacted to the destruction of war and the relativism it brought in its wake in the collections *Hostina* (Feast, 1944) and Studňa (Well, 1945). After the war, he published several collections and translated French, Hungarian, and Russian poetry.

Valentin Beniak (1894–1973)

As a student, Beniak wrote in Hungarian. After 1918, he began to publish Slovak poetry influenced by Hungarian poets (Endre Ady) and Slovak Moderna. His first collection, *Tihahnime d'alej oblaky* (Let's move on, clouds, 1928), was a great critical success. In it, he dealt with his attitude toward the Slovak heritage, the traditional way of life, anchored in the village, that was about to go through revolutionary changes. *Ozveny krokov* (The echo of steps, 1931) turned from the village world to mature reflections of individual destiny and meditations on human life. In his following four collections, Beniak broadened his horizon to comment on the world outside Slovakia (this followed travels in Italy and France), and on the social situation at home and abroad. His most sensitive reaction to the deepening crisis in Europe was expressed in *Bukvica* (Beechnut, 1938).

A patriot, Beniak identified with the nationalism of the Slovak Republic (1939–45) in his collections *Vigília* (Vigil, 1939) and *Druhá Vigília* (Second vigil, 1942); at the same time, he published verses that stand at the summit of modern Slovak poetry in the collections *Žofia* (Sophia, 1941), *Popolec* (Ash, 1942), and *Igric* (1944). The latter three collections display his technical prowess. His innovations included the use of thirteen- and twelve-syllabic dactylic and iambic verse. Žofia is an allegorical figure, representing the conscience of the age as it ineluctably approaches an apocalyptic dénouement. The war made Slovakia a plaything of the great powers that were fighting for each other's total annihilation. Žofia, a giver of life and treasury of wisdom (Sophia means "wisdom" in Greek), enabled Beniak to distance himself from the madness of the age and to dream of a golden age in which evil would be conquered and harmony restored. In *Igric,* he returned to the distant past of Slav greatness, as if to compensate for the helplessness of the present and to reaffirm traditional values at a moment when human life was seemingly worthless.

Because of his support of the regime (he worked at the ministry of interior during the war and served as president of the Union of Slovak Writers), Beniak was subsequently silenced and turned to translating, including works by Shakespeare, Goethe, Wilde, and Hungarian poets. He was allowed to return to literature only in the 1960s, when he published *Hrachor* (1967). His creative power undiminished, three more collections followed: *Plačúci Amor* (Tearful amor, 1969), *Sonety podvečerné* (Twilight sonnets, 1970), and *Medailóny a medailónky* (Medallions, 1971). While the first two are dominated by love poetry, the third is Beniak's personal and eclectic gallery of historical personalities who enriched his inner life: along with the Slovak poet Ján Hollý and the Czech novelist Božena Němcová are Leonardo da Vinci and even Spartacus. Through these personalities and his reflections on their significance, Beniak reveals the mosaic that makes up his philosophy of life, his inner credo. In this collection, he also returns to the sonnet form that he used in the 1940s.

Beniak's significance stems from his originality and classical self-sufficiency, in which he stands apart from other poets. He remains arguably the greatest poet of his generation.

Emil Boleslav Lukáč (1900–79)

In a certain sense, it is possible to see Smrek and Beniak as antipodes, and Lukáč as standing between them. He shares with Smrek a background in Protestant theology, although he did not forsake his studies, but served as a church administrator before taking up secular work. More importantly, he shared to a degree Smrek's belief in the power of female vitality and restorative power. With Beniak, he shared an interest in the classical poetic heritage of Goethe and in such French poets as Valéry and Claudel. This is obvious in his first collection, *Spoveď* (Confession, 1922). His next book, *Hymny k sláve Hosudárovej* (Hymns to the glory of the Lord, 1926), was less religious, and his third book, *O láske neláskavej* (On the unloving love, 1928) is an occasionally tortured meditation on the curses and blessings of love.

This first, most interesting and creative period of Lukáč's life ended with a rather gloomy book of verse, *Križovatky* (Crossroads, 1929), in which he drew on a number of romantic sources to deal with what seems to be a deep personal and spiritual crisis overcome by the affirmation of love. In Leipzig, during the cruel winter of his depression, Lukáč writes:

Well without water mist tossed by a storm,
o, bottomless soul, rock sliced your night.
It falls in a chasm, never touching the ground,
endless is the way into the interior.

During the 1930s, Lukáč's poetry became increasingly caught up in the deepening political crisis in Europe. The degree of his despair grew with the rise of Fascism. This gradation is observable in *Elixir* (1934), *Moloch* (1938), and *Babel* (1944). Apart from the social aspect of his poems, they also represent a personal evaluation of the poetic past, mainly his reaction to the poetry of the Moderna movement.

Like Beniak, Lukáč was not allowed to publish until the 1960s, when he re-issued some of his older poems and wrote the rhapsodic *Oda na poslednú a prvú* (Ode to the last and the first, 1967).

Laco Novomeský (1904–76)

A leading communist journalist, politician, and poet, Novomeský held high positions in the Czechoslovak government after 1948, but in 1951 his fellow communists imprisoned him on the charge of nationalism. Released in 1955, he was under a cloud well into the 1960s. He was rehabilitated in 1963, and his career took off following the Soviet invasion of 1968, when he was made the president of Matica slovenská and a member of the Central Committee of the Communist Party of Slovakia.

After publishing a book of proletarian poetry, *Nedel'a* (Sunday, 1927), Novomeský surprised his fellow travellers with *Romboid* (1932), a modernist work that used shocking juxtapositions of images, often connected through bizarre associations, and was dedicated to the memory of Janko Kráľ, a patron of all unorthodox expression. Novomeský's best poetry was collected in *Svätý za dedinou* (Saint at the end of the village, 1939). The title refers to the statue of the patron saint that villagers erected on the outskirts of their villages. Novomeský's "good simple saint,"a legendary hero, arrived in the village to help, but, seeing the vanity of his effort, turned to stone.

This work is Novomeský's reaction to the contemporary crisis, which demanded a personal commitment. The suffering he encountered during a visit to Spain during the civil war led him to meditate on the situation at home. His great accomplishment in this collection was the victory of poet over politician. The poems he published after his rehabilitation never recaptured the intensity or freedom manifested in his earlier work. Like the Czech exponent of poetism, Vítězslav Nezval, Novomeský paid dearly for the Marxist temptation, as the victory of their cause led to an artistic and personal decline.

SLOVAK SURREALISM

A movement with perhaps less far-reaching consequence than the school of lyrical prose, but much more broadly based, was the surrealist movement, in which some of Slovakia's best painters, critics, and poets took part. It was something of a protest movement, and it propelled Slovakia to cultural parity with the rest of Europe. Looked at from another angle, it was a generational movement of artists born during and immediately after the Great War, a generation much beholden to the latest literary and artistic movements emanating from the rest of Europe. Writers such as Pavol Bunčák (b. 1915), Rudolf Fábry (b. 1915), Ján Lenko (b. 1914), Vladimír Reisel (b. 1919), and Štefan Žáry (b. 1918) were educated during the first Czechoslovak Republic, unencumbered by the war and the ante-bellum status quo, young, irreverent, and of a decidedly internationalist and cosmopolitan outlook. In four almanacs published between 1938 and 1942 – during a time of world war – they paradoxically, and sometimes incomprehensibly, devoted their energies to the relativistic, exotic, and, in the opinion of many, repellent import. The result was Slovak surrealism, a poetry that, under the guise of familiar surrealist a esthetics, introduced the native landscape and found its inspiration in native predecessors, such as Kráľ. In a programmatic poem, *Plagát* (*Poster*, 1939), Reisel bragged,

> We invented the way of putting people to sleep using a dose of hashish
> To lead them to places which cause movements of all the senses
> We invented the way of changing the worlds
> We see the stars through the eyes of lunatics
> We watch the seas hovering above the cities
> We see the cities transformed into sepias

He ended the poem less than modestly:

> At our feet is the shout of future miracles

Unfortunately, Reisel's future was somewhat more prosaic: after 1945, he edited *Pravda*, and during the period of normalization, he was put in charge of the emasculated *Slovenské Pohľady*, with less than miraculous results.

Leading personalities of this genre were the poet Štefan Žáry (b. 1918), the critic Mikuláš Bakoš (1914–72), and the painter Ladislav Guderna (b. 1921). Bakoš edited three surrealist almanacs during the war and was a leading proponent of structuralism and formalism in Slovakia. Guderna became the foremost Slovak surrealist painter; after 1968, he emigrated to Canada, where he has become one of the leading artists in the Canadian surrealist group based in Vancouver, British Columbia.

Žáry is a versatile modern writer whose main form of expression is poetry, but who has penned remarkable memoirs, prose, children's literature, plays, and a great series of translations from French, Spanish, and Italian poetry. His greatest contribution to Slovak poetry is the work of his youth, collected in *Zvieratník* (Bestiary, 1941), *Stigmatizovaný vek* (Stigmatized age, 1944), *Pečať plných amfór* (The seal of full amphoras, 1944), *Pavúk pútnik* (Wandering spider, 1946), *Dobrý deň pán Villon* (Hello, Mr Villon, 1947), and *Zasľubená zem* (Promised land, 1947).

Žáry's poetry provides the answer to why surrealism was found to be the ideal vehicle for poetic and artistic expression for the generation born after the Great War. He is a poet of the uprootedness that, during the Second World War, reached apocalyptic dimensions. Apart from the dislocation of the war, surrealist Slovak poets were reacting to the accelerated process of change that they were experiencing as members of the Slovak élite. They saw their homeland swiftly transformed from a marginal territory attached to Hungary into a developed nation in the heart of Europe in the astonishingly short span of twenty years. Žáry's well-intentioned Europeanism was developed during his stay in Italy as a Slovak soldier during the Second World War, and afterwards as a journalist.

What is typical of surrealist poetics, as we know it from the French – imagery ranged according to the principle of free association, and a frontal attack against the accepted canons of aesthetics – is preserved in Slovak surrealism (also known in Slovak as *nadrealizmus*); added is a flavour imparted by the admixture of such native elements as the heritage of Slovak folk poetry and of Kráľ, and the recognizably Slovak topography. Žáry's poetry, in fact, is a unique and highly personal vision that uses surrealist poetics in the service of the native literary tradition. Thus, he writes, in *Station Death* (1944),

I will leave
I will leave on a black train of thoughts
To the cities
Which flash by like a yarn spun in winter
A man will walk up to me in midnight waiting rooms
He is an employee
Get up sir your love is leaving
Don't you hear the whistle of birds
Maybe I will open an eyelid slightly

The station'll be lit by a woman with an auburn walk
The sleep of death will overcome me
Some child will put my paralysed legs on a bench
It is awfully cold
The unheated room will foster me
It is the awful cold of hate
My train is coming
It has a fierce stormy boiler
It is already calling to me
And I will not go so that I will not have to return
It will howl like a faithful dog
For heaven's sake do not force me to gamble

The poem's surrealist elements do not prevent us from seeing the coldness of a world presented as the waiting room of a railway station, aptly called Death, a station out to claim the life of the poem's hero.

THE SIXTIES: A DECADE OF REDISCOVERY AND EXPERIMENTATION

During the first golden age of Slovak surrealism, a number of distinguished poets, such as Smrek, Beniak, and Lukáč, managed to overshadow, or at least minimize, its importance. However, the future belonged to surrealism. The poets were young enough to manage a transformation to the officially sanctioned socialist realism, while the Catholic Beniak and the Lutheran Lukáč were shunted aside for decades, to reappear, Phoenix-like, in the 1960s and 1970s, thus defying not only biology but socialist realism as well.

These poets joined the erstwhile surrealists (Žáry, Reisel, Bunčák), who, now firmly ensconced in the literary establishment, reissued their old and not-so-old surrealist works. In general, the liberal and liberating 1960s were very propitious years for surrealism. The deadening bore of the fifteen years of administrative intrusion had produced a predictable yerning for something wild and irrational. Franz Kafka, the subject of a conference in 1962 and of endless articles, became a symbol of artistic freedom, a prophet of the nightmare of bureaucratic socialism, a rallying cry for those who were silenced, intimidated, suppressed, and harrassed by the talentless incompetents of the Communist Party's administration of literature. The re-emergence of surrealism in the culture of the 1960s was a curious phenomenon that has not yet been paid due attention. It is safe to assume that the surrealists of the war years influenced significantly the generation that arrived in the 1960s.

The 1960s themselves were a turbulent decade. On the one hand, literature was gradually freed from the constraints of censorship and the worst excesses of administrative control as the Party establishment was shamed, through a series of revelations in Moscow (the Twenty-second CPSU Congress), and at home, when such publications as *Oneskorené reportáže* (Belated reports, 1962) and *Ako chutí moc* (Taste of Power, 1967) attacked the injustices of Stalinism. Written by Ladislav Mňačko, a former Stalinist, the lightly fictionalized accounts of Stalinist practices undermined the authority of the establishment and further expanded the creative space for freedom-conscious writers.

The new generation that grew up after the war experienced a schizophrenic existence during the worst years of Stalinism and entered literature just as the worst was over and, by lucky coincidence, the regime was liberalized. New possibilities for experimentation gradually opened up during the 1960s, attracting a group of talented authors. Not all of them were young; some older authors sensed that this was the time when they could get material published that earlier would have been considered unthinkable. This was the case for a fine novelist, Ladislav Ťažký (b. 1924), whose horrifying experiences on the Russian front, where he fought as a member of the Slovak army, served as the basis for his innovative, highly original prose, such as his novel *Amenmária: Samí dobrí vojaci* (Amenmaria: All the good soldiers, 1964).

What did the "newness" and "experimentation" of the 1960s mean in specifically Slovak literary conditions? The context was the collapse of the doctrine, concept, and method of socialist realism. This realism had not been retired by administrative fiat – it had been redefined for administrative purposes – but its demise was due to demoralization of the establishment following the revelations of 1956 and 1962 (at the twentieth and twenty-second CPSU congresses), and the consequent gradual pressure by the writers who constantly pushed against the limits of the permissible. The spell had been broken; although everyone still paid lip service to socialist realism, what mattered most to party officials – the control of literature – was gradually slipping from their hands, and their periodic attempts at re-establishing control were not successful: the genie was out of the bottle.

And so, while some critics still penned tributes to such model authors as František Hečko (1905–60), Peter Jilemnický (1901–49), and Fraňo Kráľ (1903–55), new writers began to appear in print who wrote in a way that was often entirely alien to these "classics," sometimes even to the extent of parodying the socialist realist models. Literary critics, led by Mikuláš Bakoš, rediscovered politically neutral formalist and structuralist criticism, resulting in the establishment of the influential Nitra School of Literary Communication.

At first, literary experimentation meant a necessary adjustment to the world outside of Slovakia, and the inevitable game of catching up with the West. Thus, Jaroslava Blažková's *Nylonový mesiac* (Nylon Moon, 1961) reminded Jozef Kot of Françoise Sagan. Anton Hykisch included in *Nadia* (1963), his prose defence of individualism and even eccentricity, references to Campanella's *The City of the Sun* and H.G. Wells's *The Shape of Things to Come.* The influence of French existentialist writing was particularly strong in the work of Ján Johanides, as evidenced in *Súkromie* (Privacy, 1963). Nevertheless, František Miko praised Johanides for his independence, analysis, and rare tone. Such characteristics were a far cry from the formerly desirable positive hero, class struggle, and radiant light of the bright, imminent future. One of the popular voices of contemporary fiction, Peter Jaroš, published an imitative novel, *Váhy* (Scales, 1966), a work heavily indebted to the French *nouveau roman.* The most promising author of the younger generation of the 1960s, Vincent Šikula, made an impressive début with a collection of stories entitled *Povetrie* (Atmosphere, 1968). Paradoxically, anticipating this process of gradual liberalization, which was so beneficial for the generation responsible for the experimentation of the 1960s, was Dominik Tatarka, the author of *The Demon of Conformism* (1956).

Dominik Tatarka (1913–89)

Tatarka's roots were in the surrealist movement, which he discovered while he was studying French at the Sorbonne. His first work was published in 1935, and in 1942 he surprised critics with *V úzkosti hľadania* (Search in despair), an experimental ensemble of tales that was a forerunner of his much more ambitious surrealist novel, *Panna zázračnica* (Wondrous virgin, 1944). This work prefigures what was to become the definitive Tatarka approach to prose: fragmentation, reflection, and a revelatory tendency that, together, had a liberating quality. Reading Tatarka meant learning not so much about his characters, but about the world, about a definite segment of contemporary intellectual history, and about the narrator.

The novel *Farská republika* (Parish republic, 1948) is a thorough demolition of the Slovak Republic (1939–45). It explains what a significant number of Slovak intellectuals disliked about the regime: that a somewhat provincial, limited mentality had gained access to power and exercised it as a seemingly divine mandate. Only eight years later, Tatarka had the honour to have been among the first to denounce a much more universal evil.

The Demon of Conformism (1956) was one of the most outspoken literary works published in eastern Europe at the time. Having attacked the very basis of the regime's stability – conformism produced by fear – Tatarka analyzed what conformism meant for literature in general, and for the writer in particular. In a first-person narrative by a recently deceased author, Tatarka used the grotesque (a device left over from the surrealist period) to present a vicious and astonishingly outspoken critique of the mindlessness of conformism and the ever-present lie maintained by the communist regime. Such honesty did not reappear in Czechoslovakia until the end of the 1960s, when Slovak writers were becoming more open – encouraged, no doubt, by the Soviet dissident movement spearheaded among writers by Alexander Solzhenitsyn. However, Tatarka himself, having fallen out of favour with the authorities in 1968, spent his last twenty years as an ostracized writer, supported only by the small dissident community in Bratislava and Prague and publishing in samizdat.

Stripped of his life of privilege and meeting his erstwhile friends and acquaintances (now the leading members of political and cultural life) only accidentally, Tatarka became Slovakia's most prominent literary dissident. Artistically, his stand as a defiant outsider proved quite liberating, and he profited from his position by writing his most uninhibited and controversial work, *Písačky* (Writings) in the mid-1970s, publishing it abroad. This work is a necessary, though excessively – even pathologically – erotic appendix to "official" prose, which was recovering from the shell-shock it had suffered after the forceful suppression of freedom perpetrated in 1968.

NORMALIZATION (1969–89)

After 1968, the new regime, which came to power with Soviet help and was led by President Gustav Husák, formulated a policy of "normalization," which meant the re-establishment of administrative control over the arts and the press, with the attendant loss of freedoms attained during the 1960s. There were new purges. A comparison with the situation in Bohemia is instructive. Czech literature was seriously damaged as many of its outstanding representatives were silenced after 1968, and some chose to go into exile. In Slovakia, however, the regime used rewards as well as punishments.

The process of federalization opened a new chapter in national life, and some men of literature now stood at the forefront of national culture. This complicated situation was elucidated in Miroslav Kusý's "Slovak Phenomenon" (1985), in which he referred to the fact that, in contrast to those in Bohemia, writers in Slovakia were preoccupied with achieving nationalist rather than political aims. They suddenly reaped benefits by being appointed to ministerial positions (the poet

Miroslav Válek became minister of culture) or lucrative and prestigious offices (the novelist Vladimir Mináč became the president of Matica slovenská and a member of the Central Committee of the Communist Party of Slovakia). Vladimir Mináč (b. 1922) is known as the author of the novelistic trilogy *Generácia* (Generation, 1958, 1959, 1961), but he will no doubt be remembered for the remarkable essays that won him many admirers at home and abroad, particularly *Dúchanie do pahrieb* (Blowing on the embers, 1970) and *Zobrané spory Jozefa Miloslava Hurbana* (Collected arguments of Jozef Miloslav Hurban, 1974), in which he brilliantly uncovered for his contemporaries the glory and tragedy of the nineteenth-century revivalist movement.

It is true that during the great Catholic demonstration in the spring of 1988, known as Sviečkový pochod (the candle procession), some of the poets who identified with the regime, such as Válek and Vojtech Mihálik, praised the violent police suppression of this peaceful event, in which Catholics gave vent to their forty-year-old frustration with the anti-Catholic policy of the regime. Those who did not identify with the reform movement of 1968, or those who publicly recanted their participation in it, were also welcomed into the new establishment. In addition, many of the more talented writers of the 1960s were too young to have been involved politically; fewer still were communists, and they thus could not actively identify with the Dubček era.

Ján Johanides, Antoń Hykisch, Peter Jaroš, and Vincent Šikula matured in the 1970s, when their most important works to date appeared: Johanides, in *Nepriznané vrany* (Unreported crows, 1978), analyzes the tragedy of man's uncaring attitude toward the environment and meditates on the deeper connections between ecology and its impact on society. Hykisch excelled in *Čas Majstrov* (The time of the masters, 1977). Jaroš's *Tisícročná včela* (Millennial bee, 1979) is a historical novel dealing with the pre-1918 years; it is an imaginative and sensual work reminiscent of the Latin American "magical realism" school, for which the Slovak novel had an affinity through its native lyrical prose. Unfortunately, the novel suffers because of Jaroš's attempt to satisfy the censor with an official (and therefore distorted) account of crucial historical events. Finally, Šikula's trilogy *Majstri, Muškát, Vilma* (1976, 1977, 1979) depicts Slovakia's controversial history over the previous fifty years. The tension between historical, distorted, and popular perceptions of the historical changes was such that an orthodox Marxist critic, Daniel Okáli, found the trilogy unacceptable.

These writers and others (such as Puškáš, Ballek, Sloboda, and, from the older generation, the novelist Alfonz Bednár [1914–89] managed to preserve a degree of creative integrity throughout the 1970s. This was particularly true of Ladislav Ballek.

Ladislav Ballek (b. 1941)

Trained as a teacher, Ballek soon moved into radio and journalism, becoming an editor at the prestigious publishing house Slovenský spisovateľ in 1972. His first work was published in 1964, but his subsequent three books comprised a period of apprenticeship, which was necessary for the development of his substantial talent, although he suffered needlessly from a certain insecurity. He came through this process greatly strengthened.

Južná pošta (Southern mail, 1974) demonstrates not only Ballek's true voice, but his major theme as well. It is a fictional autobiography that highlights a rather neglected Slovak region, Southern Slovakia, a battleground of ethnic loyalties and a place of painful historical memories. He portrays it as a region where Magyars and Slovaks change status, reflecting the shifting political realities of the nation itself.

Ballek was particularly interested in the fate of the Slovaks, the original inhabitants of the region, who would return to it after being repeatedly forced out by the Magyars. Their sad fate is at the centre, though not always obviously, of his elaborate narrative structure. He sustained this theme in a loose trilogy of novels: after *Južná pošta*, *Pomocník* (Assistant, 1977) and *Agáty* (Acacias, 1983).

Ballek resisted emotionalism, and his well-balanced ensemble is a marvel of rational fictional construction. Once readers fully enters his world, they sense the subtleties of the text. Within the broad epic strokes of his story-telling is an inner world full of psychological and historical echoes, allusions, and meanings. These enrich the novels without hindering the narrative.

Ballek wrote with a great deal of freedom despite the new witch-hunt, which resulted in the suppression of nonconformists such as Tatarka. If he manages to preserve the territory he has carved for himself with his great novels, he will emerge as the leading novelist of the last decade of this century. In poetry, a similar position might be held by Milan Rúfus.

Milan Rúfus (b. 1928)

Since it is unlikely that someone unexpected will overshadow the established poets by the end of the 1990s, the remaining years of this century might very well confirm Rúfus's position as its pre-eminent Slovak poet. Born in a village near Liptovský Mikuláš, where he attended high school, Rúfus studied Slovak and history at Comenius University, in Bratislava, and he remained there to teach after completing his doctorate in 1952.

He started publishing in periodicals in 1944, but his first book, *Až dozrieme* (When we mature), did not appear until 1956. This work was immediately seen as the product of a fully mature major poet. Seen against the backdrop of the pathetic poetry of socialist realism, Rúfus's book was controversial:

Poem
Life breaks on a sharp edge of a dagger.
Therein lies its tragedy,
There is its triumph. Flowers rain on monuments.
The poet's mouth sings:

– Again a pain gave birth to tears.
It threw them into the face of the public. –
And what is truth? A fairy-tale good witch,
who forever escapes us.

Rúfus's emergence can be understood as a reaction both to the modernistic stream that produced surrealism and to sterile socialist realism. His sophisticated poetry demands much of the reader, for he is a master of mood and creates an ambience that is uniquely his own. It is difficult to trace a single clear influence on his work, but a careful acquaintanceship with the major French symbolists, the Russian poets of the 1920s, and the Czech and Slovak poets of this century is obvious, although Rufus's poetry is far from derivative.

The book *Chlapec* (Boy, 1966) and *Chlapec maľuje dúhu* (Boy paints a rainbow, 1974) written much earlier but published only after considerable delay, confirmed and enhanced Rúfus's reputation as a major new voice in Slovak poetry. *Zvony* (Bells, 1968) and *Triptych* (1969) marked a new stage in his work. He developed an intimate voice, which he uses in a form of a fictional dialogue with the reader, whom he address as a confidant:

In the Land of Nobody
My poem hurts me, my brother. It hurts.
The silence of the galley echoes in it and hurts.
And time and time and a cicada in the watch …

Outside, sadness rains like stars on the barns,
on the empty words depopulated by God.

And you retreat into no man's land.
For silence, silence which does not rumble
with words, that hollow crutch of mankind.

In the late 1960s and early 1970s, Rúfus turned his attention to pictorial art. He created a number of works in which his poems illustrate a number of paintings or photographs, and vice versa: *Ľudia v horách* (People in the mountains, 1969), *Kolíska* (Cradle, 1972), *Hľadanie obrazu* (Search for a painting, 1973, with the artist M.A. Bazovský), and *Hudba tvarov* (Music of the shapes, 1977, with the artist Ľudovít Fulla).

Like many poets before him, Rúfus rediscovered the magical world of the folk-tales collected by Pavol Dobšinský in the nineteenth century. The result was *Kniha rozprávok* (A book of fairy-tales, 1975).

The publication of a selection of Rúfus's best poetry, *Básne* (Poems, 1975), confirmed his reputation as a great poet. Very little of his writing, even the most topical, has dated. Paradoxically, his strength is often in the meekness and humility of his Christian religiosity, which shines luminously from his modest stanzas:

> *Message*
> We don't know what is in us. Where is the source of the water in our hand and the tear on our cheek.
>
> We don't know what is in us. And the poets look for the source, idiots; they will kill that snowflake on an inquisitive hand.

While some young writers were able to publish by observing the limits of the permissible, there one group of writers were banned and another group started to publish samizdat literature. In the banned group, in addition to Tatarka, were older authors who made their name before 1968: H. Ponická, I. Kadlečík, P. Hrúz, A. Marenčin, M. Hamada, and S. Čechová. Hana Ponická presented a longer list of proscribed authors in a speech at the Third Congress of Slovak Writers in Bratislava (March 3, 1977). The resulting persecution of this courageous woman inspired her to write, for the record, *Lukavické zápisky* (Lukavica notes, 1989), a samizdat book published in Toronto.

Also in the samizdat group is Martin Šimečka (b. 1956), the most successful of the small number of young Slovak dissident writers who published in unofficially printed journals. Šimečka's novel *Džin* (1990; an English translation, *The Year of the Frog*, [1993] was published by the Louisiana University Press) was successful in its French translation and won the prestigious Pegasus Prize for Literature awarded by the Mobil Corporation as the first Slovak literary work that caught the attention of the English-speaking world. *Džin*, a sort of postmodernist *Bildungsroman*, consists of three novellas that follow the maturing process of Milan, whose dissident father is in prison and whose mother is giving up on life. The reflective narrator introduces us to the world of "normalization" from which he can escape only to his lover Tania, to work in the surgical ward of a hospital, and to his meditations. The bitter conclusion confirms the hero's will to live and struggle for a normal existence, though he is surrounded by people who are either resigned to or unconscious of their predicament.

Nevertheless, though this unofficial, independent literature is a rightful component of Slovak literature, it would be fair to say, as Kusý suggests in his essay "*Slovenský fenomén*" (Slovak phenomenon, 1985), that it was less significant than the independent literature in Bohemia precisely because, until very recently, the energies of Slovak writers were oriented toward grasping national rather than political dimensions of life. This orientation meant that the best writers did not emigrate after 1968, as did their Czech equivalents. The exile of Škvorecký, Salivarová, Kohout, Kundera, Lustig, and others was a great boon to Czech literature, popularizing it and making it internationally known. In Slovakia, young and unorthodox voices were occasionally permitted to publish, as was the case with the very talented Dušan Mitana, Rudolf Sloboda, and Pavel Vilikovský.

LITERATURE IN EXILE

No matter whether it is written at home or abroad, officially or unofficially, Slovak language poetry, prose, and drama belongs to the Slovak nation, as is now recognized by the new political establishment in Bratislava. However, this belated recognition is unlikely to be helpful to those who went into exile, were ostracized for forty years, and died unrecognized in their homeland.

There is a tradition of Slovak literature written in exile. One of the greatest Slovak novelists, Martin Kukučín, wrote abroad, in Croatia and Chile. The greatest twentieth-century slovak novelist, J.C. Hronský, wrote his masterpiece, *Andreas Búr, the Master*, in Rome and Argentina. There were others.

There have been three waves of emigration since 1945. The first consisted mainly of those who identified with the Slovak Republic and left in 1945; the second wave emigrated after the communists seized power in 1948 and included those opposed to the nationalist regime, except, of course, for the communists themselves; the third group left after the invasion of Czechoslovakia in 1968. This was the most diversified group, including communists who identified with the reforms crushed by Soviet tanks.

Quite a sizeable group of Slovak writers and intellectuals emigrated after 1945. A significant group of the leading officers of Matica slovenská (S. Mečiar, F. Hrušovský, H. Bartek, J. Cincík, K. Geraldini) left with Hronský, as did a group of young poets (R. Dilong, M. Šprinc, K. Strmeň, J. Okáľ). Many of them continued writing and publishing, though no one was more prolific than the Franciscan priest Rudolf Dilong (1905–86).

An unusual poet and *enfant terrible* before the war, Dilong published several collections of poetry almost every year. His Franciscan religiosity had a surrealist cast when this movement was the leading vehicle of poetic expression. After his emigration to Argentina, in 1947, and later to the United States, his themes were the lyrical glorification of patriotism, in *Diaľky bez domova* (Far away and homeless, 1950); the poetic archaeology of the beginnings of Christianity in Slovakia, in *Slovo Božie* (Word of God, 1955); and, increasingly in his last years, mysticism and prophecy, in *Vidím otvorené nebo* (I see the open sky, 1976).

Along with Karol Strmeň, the Benedictine priest Mikuláš Šprinc (1914–86) turned Cleveland into a centre of Slovak culture during a time (the 1950s) of great cultural stagnation at home. Šprinc's first works were translations of Rilke and of Italian poetry. He was charmed by the nature of the New World, and his poetry collections – *Na Floride sám* (Alone in Florida, 1953) and *Cesty a osudy* (Travels and destinies, 1957), commenting on his trip to California – reflected this. He used the harmony and deceptive simplicity of the sonnet for an evocation of and paean to beauty in *Sonety o kráse* (Sonnets about beauty, 1976).

A linguistic genius who, as a professor in the United States, astonished his students with his knowledge of languages and photographic memory, which allowed him to quote poetry in many languages by heart, Karol Strmeň (b. 1921) is best known as the most prolific Slovak translator of poetry. Rilke, Dante, Petrarch, Poe, T. S. Eliot, and Francis Thompson, among others, found in Strmeň a translator of unusual linguistic facility, poetic invention, and judiciousness. Strmeň's *Strieborná Legenda* (Silver legend) and a cycle of poems published in 1950, *Putovné piesne* (Wandering songs) betray both mature talent and youthful exuberance. His main accomplishment lies in the meditative lyrical poetry collected in *Čakajú nivy jar* (Fields await spring, 1963) and *Znamenie ryby* (The sign of the fish, 1969). His contribution to Marian spirituality was collected in the book *Preblahoslavená* (Most blessed of all, 1977).

The emigrant wave of 1948 included the poets Gorazd Zvonický, F. Hrtús-Jurina, and Andrej Žarnov (a prominent nationalist poet); fine literary critics and essayists such as Imrich Kružliak (a publisher of the best Slovak paper abroad, *Horizont*); Jozef Špetko, a leading Slovak intellectual historian; and František Vnuk, a historian who wrote a history of socialist realism in literature (*Sedemnásť neúrodnych rokov* [Seventeen wasted years], 1965). The events of 1968 precipitated the departure of such established Slovak writers as Ladislav Mňačko, Jaroslava Blažková, Agneša Gundová-Jergová, and Rudolf Skukálek, as well as those who would start their careers in exile, including Irena Brežná and Emil Knieža. Those who left after 1968 had to wait for twenty years to hear the good news from the literary establishment in Slovakia that there was but one literature, exile or no exile. For most of those who left their homeland in the more vicious years, 1945 and 1948, the news came too late. Many of the leading writers of that generation, including Hronský, Dilong, and Šprinc, were already dead. But so was totalitarian control of literature. In the final analysis, a prophetic statement by the persecuted Russian writer Mikhail Bulgakov holds true: manuscripts do not burn. From the United States, Canada, Argentina, Australia, and western Europe, manuscripts are coming home from their exile.

There is, after all, but one Slovak literature.

Conclusion

The history of Slovak literature embraced in the twentieth century a similar compass as did that of Czech literature following the national renaissance of the 1840s. However, Slovak literature was animated by a different set of requirements. Once Czech literature was adopted by the educated Czech élite, its existence was assured and it met with increasing success, recently becoming acclaimed internationally. Comparatively, Slovak literature cannot boast such recognition.

Yet Slovak writers believe that the long-pursued goal of parity with other cultures has been achieved. This was the consensus at an international conference in London, England, in 1987, the first devoted to Slovak prose of the previous thirty years. It remains to be seen if this accomplishment will set the stage for the appearance of a powerful artistic personality whose voice will overcome national barriers. It is quite possible that such a literary voice is among us already, in the person of a Ladislav Ballek, a Milan Rúfus, or someone as yet unrecognized. This would go long way toward answering the self-critical observation of Štefan Krčméry, who despaired to find among his contemporaries an author who could manage to write a novel.

Indeed, the study of Slovak literary history is instructive in how the territory covered by Slovak literature extended so far in such a relatively short time. Štefan Krčméry (1892–1955), it bears stressing, started his career as an administrator of Matica slovenská under Jaroslav Vlček, whose *History of Slovak Literature* (1889–90) he set out to correct in his own *History of Slovak Literature*, published posthumously, in 1976. Krčméry's work contains an original thesis on the origin and function of poetry, and it concentrates on poets because Krčméry was a poet himself. But it is not apologetic in the sense that Vlček's work was: Vlček, after all, was trying to prove to the Czechs that a *separate* Slovak literature *existed*. Krčméry's literary history concerns the quality of the literature as well. Andrej Mráz (1904–64) presents Slovak literature to the foreign reader in *Die Literatur der Slowaken* (1943), already assuming its quality and defending its place among the other European literatures during a time when the existence of some of those nations was itself in doubt. After the Second World War, forty years passed before the appearance of *Dejiny slovenskej literatúry: od stredoveku po súčasnosť* (History of Slovak literature: From the middle ages to the present, 1988), by Stanislav Šmatlák (b. 1925), in which the dead hand of political expediency is kept away until the twentieth century. This represents a further important milepost in the achievement of Slovak historiography. Šmatlák also pays due credit to his predecessors and to such outstanding contemporary critics as Alexander Matuška (1910–75), Ján Števček (b. 1929), and Vladimír Petrík (b. 1929).

It is clear that much has been done to illuminate the past and understand the present. Following the recent Velvet Revolution, one can reasonably expect even more from Slovak literature and criticism. It should try to extricate itself from its isolation and introduce itself to the rest of the world.

Presently, the only Slovak literaty works available in English are Hronský's *Jozef Mak*, translated by Andrew Činčura, the editor of an anthology of Slovak literature and Kukučín's and Slančíková-Timrava's short stories, translated by Norma Leigh Rudinsky, the author of a study of Slovak women writers. Much has to be done in the West. First of all, the appearance of English translations of some representative *contemporary* Slovak authors, such as Ballek and Rúfus, is long overdue. Promising in this respect may be the appearance of Šimečka's *The Year of the Frog*. Good-quality English translations of the best Slovak novels of the last fifteen years would enrich world literature and demonstrate that the literary strivings of Slovakia have not been unavailing.

Literary history has its own dynamics, but it is by no means immune to great historical changes. The years 1848, 1918, and 1989 provided Slovak writers with new openings and opportunities for far-reaching artistic experimentation, and the means to survive in difficult times and, finally, to flourish. The changes of 1848 and 1918 were heralded by great historical events originating far from Slovakia proper. Similarly, the Velvet Revolution of 1989, which received its impetus from decisions made elsewhere, offers yet another opening and the promise of a liberal cultural policy, this time guaranteed by democracy. And with Slovakia independent, it may well be on the verge of a cultural renaissance.

Slovak literature will react in its own time to historical events. It has a solid base on which to build and the experience to venture beyond its borders, and beyond the borders of the Slavic world. When this happens, it will not be due to political expediency, or to the celebrity status accorded to dissidents, but because of work of a quality and wealth of imagination that will capture the attention of all those who have yet to discover this perennial Cinderella of central European literature.

Bibliography

SOURCES IN ENGLISH

Bakhtin, M.M. *Problems of Dostoevsky's Poetics.* Translated by R.W. Rotsel. Ann Arbor: Ardis 1973.

Brock, Peter. *The Slovak National Awakening.* Toronto: University of Toronto Press 1976.

Burckhardt, Jacob. *Civilization of the Renaissance in Italy.* New York: Signet 1960.

Dvorník, F. *Byzantine Missions Among the Slavs.* New Brunswick, NJ: Rutgers University Press 1970.

Kirschbaum, J.M. *Slovak Language and Literature.* Winnipeg: University of Manitoba 1975.

Kramoris, Ivan J. *An Anthology of Slovak Poetry.* Cleveland: Benedictine High School 1947.

Kružliak, Imrich. "A Quarter Century of Slovak Culture: 1945–1970." In J.M. Kirschbaum, ed., *Slovakia in the 19th & 20th Centuries,* 171–99. Toronto: SWC Press 1973.

Lacko, Michael. *Sts Cyril and Methodius.* 2nd ed. Rome: Slovak Editions 1969.

Manning, C.A. *An Anthology of Czech and Slovak Poetry.* New York: Columbia University Press 1929.

Petro, Peter. "Slovak Surrealist Poetry." *Prism International* (Summer–Fall 1976): 146–64.

Pynsent, Robert B., ed. *Modern Slovak Prose: Fiction Since 1954.* London: Macmillan 1990.

Rudinsky, N. *Incipient Feminists: Women Writers in the Slovak National Revival.* Columbus, OH: Slavica 1991.

Sabo, Gerald J., ed. *Valaská Škola, by Hugolín Gavlovič.* Columbus: Slavica 1987.

Selver, Paul. *A Century of Czech and Slovak Poetry.* London: New Europe Publishing Co. 1946.

Slovakia. Special issue on Slovak Literature. Edited by Norma Leigh Rudinsky. Vol. 30, nos 55–56 (1982–83).

Šmatlák, Stanislav. *Hviezdoslav: A National and World Poet.* Bratislava: Obzor 1969.

Števček, Pavol. *Contemporary Slovak Literature.* Translated by Olga Horská. Bratislava: Obzor 1980.

Timrava, B.S. *That Alluring Land: Slovak Stories.* Translated by N. Rudinsky. Pittsburgh: Pittsburgh University Press 1992.

SOURCES IN OTHER LANGUAGES

Ambrus, J. *Ján Hollý očami svojich súčasníkov.* Bratislava: SVKL 1964.

Bakoš, Mikuláš. *Vývin slovenského verša od školy Štúrovej.* Bratislava: SAV 1966.

Bálent, B. *Piesne Jána Silvána.* Martin: Matica slovenská 1957.

Ballová, J. "Chronológia autorkinho života a diela." In L'udmila Podjavorinská, ed., *Dielo.* Bratislava: Tatran, 1987.

Brtáň, R. *Historické spevy a piesne.* Bratislava: Tatran 1978.

Chmel, R. *Dejiny v dejinách.* Bratislava: Slovenský spisovateľ 1981.

Chyzhevskyi, D. *Štúrova filozófia života.* Bratislava: SUS 1941.

Cvrkal, I. *S.H. Vajanský a nemecká literatúra.* Bratislava: Veda 1984.

Čepan, O. "Janko Kráľ': *Zborník statí,* 103–92. Bratislava: Tatran, 1976.

– *Kontúry naturizmu.* Bratislava: Slovenský spisovateľ 1977.

Černý, V. *Stredoveká dráma.* Bratislava: SVKL 1964.

Dekan, J. *Veľká Morava.* 2nd ed. Bratislava: Tatran 1979.

Dvorník, F. *Les Légendes de Constantine et Methode vues de Byzance.* Hattiesburg, MS: Academic International 1989.

Eliáš, M. "Peter Benický a jeho slovenské verše." In P. Benický, *Slovenské verše.* Bratislava: Tatran 1981.

Felix, J. "Ivan Krasko na pozadí francúzskeho symbolizmu." *Litteraria,* 20–21 (1978–79): 130–53.

Gáfrik, M. *Poézia slovenskej moderny.* Bratislava: SAV 1965.

Grivec, Franz. *Konstantin und Method Lehrer der Slaven.* Wiesbaden: O. Harrassowitz 1960.

Hamada, M. *Od baroka ku klasicizmu.* Bratislava: SAV 1967.

Handzová, Želmíra, ed. *Múdrost a skromnosť idú spolu: Elena Maróthy Šoltésová.* Martin: Osveta 1989.

Holotíkova, Z. *Ladislav Novomeský.* Bratislava: Pravda 1980.

Kochol, V. *Poézia štúrovcov.* Bratislava: SAV 1955.

– *Problémy a postavy slovenskej obrodeneckej literatúry.* Bratislava: SAV 1965.

Kopčan, S. *Jozef Miloslav Hurban: Sborník.* Bratislava: Osvetový ústav 1967.

Kotvan, I., ed. *Bernolákovské polemiky.* Bratislava: SAV 1966.

Kraus, C. *Poézia Jána Bottu.* Bratislava: Tatran 1981.

– , ed. *Na lútnu.* Bratislava: Tatran 1986.

Krčméry, S. *Zo slovenskej hymnológie.* Liptovský Mikuláš: Tranoscius 1936.

– *Dejiny literatúry slovenskej.* 2 vols. Bratislava: Tatran 1976.

Kučera, M. *Postavy veľkomoravskej histórie.* Martin: Osveta 1986.

– "Vajanského román *Letiace tiene.*" *Slovenská literatúra,* 33 (1986): 105–26.

Lesňáková, S. *Slovenská a ruská próza.* Bratislava: Veda 1983.

Litteraria 16. *Literárny romantizmus.* Bratislava 1974.

Marčok, V. *Počiatky slovenskej novodobej prózy.* Bratislava: SAV 1968.

Matuška, Alexander. *Osobnosti.* Bratislava: Slovenský Spisovateľ 1973.

Miko, F. "Funkčný a výrazový synkretizmus v barokovej literatúre." *Litteraria* 13 (1971): 194–231.

Mináč. V. *Dúchanie do pahrieb.* Bratislava: Smena 1970.

– *Zobrané spory Jozefa Miloslava Hurbana.* Bratislava 1974.

– *Portréty.* Bratislava: Smena 1986.

– *Súvislosti.* Bratislava: Slovenský spisovateľ 1976.

Minárik, J., ed. *Slovenská renezančna lútna. Antológia so slovenskej renezančnej poézie.* Bratislava: Tatran 1982.

– *Baroková literatúra. Svetová, česká, slovenská.* Bratislava: SPN 1984.

– *Dejiny slovenskej literatúry.* Vol. 1 *Staršia slovenska literatúra.* Bratislava: SPN 1985.

– *Renezančná a humanistická literatúra. Svetová, česká, slovenská.* Bratislava: SPN 1985.

– *Z klenotnice staršieho slovenského písomníctva.* Vol. 2, *Antológia renezančných a humanistických literárnych textov.* Bratislava: Tatran 1985.

Mišianik, J. *Pohľady do staršej slovenskej literatúry.* Bratislava: Veda 1974.

– *Antológia staršej slovenskej literatúry.* 2nd ed. Bratislava: SAV 1981.

Mráz, Andrej. *Dejiny slovenskej literatúry.* ed. Bratislava: SAV 1948.

– *Medzi našimi literatúrami.* Bratislava: SVKL 1960.

Noge, J. *Martin Kukučín tradicionalista a novátor.* Bratislava: SAV 1962.

– *Slovenská romantická próza.* Bratislava: SAV 1969.

Noge, J. *Podoby realizmu v medzivojnovej proze. Od sociálnej reality k socialistickému realizmu.* Bratislava: Slovenský spisovateľ 1983.

Noskovič, A. *Ján Chalúpka, tvorca slovenskej veselohry.* Bratislava: SAV 1955.

Palkovič, P. *Dialógy s Tajovským.* Bratislava: Tatran 1982.

Pašteka, J. "Dramatická tvorba Pavla Socháňa." *Slovenské divadlo,* 15 (1968): 169–82; 16 (1969): 302–22.

– "Umelecké princípy Hviezdoslavovej dramatiky." *Slovenské divadlo,* 27 (1979): 273–338.

Paulíny, E. *Slovesnosť a kultúrny jazyk Veľkej Moravy.* Bratislava: SVKL 1964.

– *Dejiny spisovnej slovenčiny od začiatkov po súčasnosť.* Bratislava: SPN 1983.

Petrík, Vladimír. *Hľadanie prítomneho času.* Bratislava: Smena 1970.

– *Človek v Jégého diele.* Bratislava: Tatran 1979.

Petrů, E. *Zašifrovaná skutečnost.* Ostrava: Profil 1972.

Pišút, M. *Počiatky básnickej školy Štúrovej.* Bratislava: Učená spoločnosť Šafáriková 1938.

– *Básnik Janko Kráľ a jeho Dráma sveta.* Turčiansky sv. Martin: Matica slovenská 1948.

Pražák. A. *S Hviezdoslavom.* Bratislava: SVKL 1995.

Rampák, Z. *K charakteru štúrovskej drámy.* Turčiansky sv. Martin: Matica Slovenska 1947.

Slavkovská, G., ed. *Ja miluji, nesmím povídati …* Bratislava: Tatran 1977.

Škultéty, Jozef. *Stodvadsaťpäť rokov zo slovenského života.* Martin: Matica slovenská 1920.

Šmatlák, S. "Význam básnických počiatkov Pavla Országha Hviezdoslava pre vývin slovenskej poézie." *Slovenská literatúra,* 2 (1955): 249–304.

– "Vznik a vývin nadrealizmu." *Slovenská literatúra,* 13 (1967): 22–31, 123–47.

– *Vývin a tvar Kraskovej lyriky.* Bratislava: Tatran 1976.

– *Dve storočia slovenskej lyriky.* Bratislava: Tatran 1979.

– *Dejiny slovenskej literatúry od stredoveku po súčasnosť*. Bratislava: Tatran 1988.

Šmatlak, S., ed. *Hviezdoslav zblízka. Výber z listov.* Bratislava: Tatran 1985.

– *Esej o slovenskom románe. Od realizmu k naturalizmu.* Bratislava: Tatran 1979.

– *Moderný slovenský román.* Bratislava: Tatran 1983.

– *Súčasný slovenský román,* Bratislava: Tatran 1987.

Števček, Ján. *Lyrizovaná próza.* Bratislava: Tatran 1973.

Šútovec, M. *Romány a mýty.* Bratislava: Tatran 1982.

Tibenský, J. *Chvály a obrany slovenského národa.* Bratislava, 1965.

– *Veľká ozdoba Uhorska.* Bratislava: Tatran 1984.

Urbancová, H., and C. Kraus, eds. *Antológia literárnovedných textov obdobia národnebo obrodenia.* Bratislava: Univerzita Komenského 1982.

Vlček, Jaroslav. *Dejiny literatúry slovenskej.* 1890. Bratislava: Slovenské vydavateľstvo krásnej literatúry 1953.

Vyvíjalová, M. *Mladý Ján Hollý.* Bratislava: Tatran 1975.

– *Juraj Palkovič (1769–1850).* Bratislava: SAV 1968.

Votrubová, S. *Živena: jej osudy a práca.* Martin: Živena 1931.

Wollman, S. "Historické a štruktúrne spoločenstvo starých slovanských literatúr." *Slovenská literatúra* 34 (1987): 1–12.

Zambor, J. *Ivan Krasko a poézia českej moderny.* Bratislava: Tatran 1981.

Index